Leadership
The Journey Inward

Fourth Edition

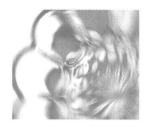

Delorese Ambrose, Ed.D.

KENDALL/HUNT PUBLISHING COMPANY
4050 Westmark Drive   Dubuque, Iowa 52002

*Motivation is a fire from within. If someone else tries to
light that fire under you, chances are it will burn briefly.*

—Stephen Covey

Contents

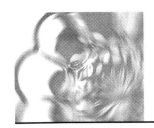

Foreword

The reactions to *Leadership: The Journey Inward* have far exceeded my expectations. I continue to receive positive feedback and helpful ideas from my readers in business, education, government, and health care. A client at PNC Bank recently told me he felt the book is even more relevant today than when he first read it. I'm told that a valedictorian at a recent college graduation ceremony brought the book to the podium, held it up, and proclaimed that it had made a difference in his life. These votes of confidence have given me courage to revisit this work and infuse it with new energy. This fourth edition has been lovingly shaped by feedback from readers throughout the U.S. and as far away as the University of Cairo, in Egypt.

In this latest edition, I have added a chapter on trust and trustworthiness that explores in great detail what trust is, how we gain it or lose it, and what behaviors and character traits make a leader trustworthy. Again, I encourage you to get a special journal and take the time to write your honest responses to the questions at the end of each chapter before moving on to the next one. By allowing you to *journey inward* in an experiential, rather than theoretical, way, I am confident this journaling exercise will deepen your self-awareness and support your leadership development. You might also find it useful to go through the process with a learning partner or coach.

DA

Acknowledgments

When I wrote the first edition of this book in 1991, I was deeply influenced by the teachings of two of my most cherished mentors, who encouraged me to capture my thoughts in writing. The late Kaleel Jamison constantly reminded me *"if you don't like the world the way you find it, you must change it."* My friend and colleague Janet Hagberg insisted—and still does—that *"true leadership begins when you are willing to be someone other than who the world wants you to be."* As I write this fourth edition, I remain grateful for their wise counsel that still enriches my life and my understanding of leadership.

I am also deeply grateful to Dr. Richard Friend, my dear friend and collaborator who insisted that I stop referring to this as my "little book" and celebrate its many gifts, and to Donna Bennett for your friendship and sage coaching through *The Leadership Journey Program for High Achieving Women at Midlife.* My days with you on the leadership development path have been most rewarding.

Special thanks to my many clients, business and government, and the Institute of Management Studies (IMS), for your confidence in my abilities and your willingness to engage me in your change efforts. This book's for you.

Delorese Ambrose, October 2007

Introduction

> *Experience, which destroys innocence, also leads one back to it.*
>
> —JAMES BALDWIN

Since the writing of the first edition of *Leadership: The Journey Inward*, I have grown in both humility and conviction. I am more aware of how little I know and am more open to learning. At the same time, I am clearer about what I do believe and more willing to go to bat for the values that I am passionate about. This paradox of not knowing and yet believing; of simultaneous confusion and clarity of purpose has led me on a renewed search for a deeper understanding of personal and organizational effectiveness. It has also sharpened my understanding of leadership and my commitment to working with those who want to "change their world" for the better. Along the way, I have met many new teachers and revisited some old ones.

Perhaps the most important of these teachers has been my own life. In my quest to develop myself as a leader in my field, I came face to face with a crisis of integrity ten years ago. I had been logging many days on the road, moving with easy access between various enterprises. I was offering seminars in business and government, partnering with clients to launch diversity initiatives, conducting culture audits, facilitating team-building retreats, writing, waking up in strange hotels and forgetting which city I was in, returning home for brief stints, and starting over again.

Through it all I was losing perspective. Yet, irony of all ironies, I was educating executives and professionals on how to forge change and restore equilibrium in their workplaces and their work lives. In framing my work experience, I had become attached to the routine of moving from task to task, client to client, and city to city, and was becoming detached from the deeper meaning of my work.

Then, out of the blue, as brilliant writer Zora Neale Hurston once put it, "something fell off the shelf inside of me." This inner shift was a clear call to go deeper. I was forced to stop in my tracks and examine my life and my work. I had to look at the concepts I taught in a new and deeply personal light. The flood of questions that sweep into our psyches when we are being called to deepen our experience of living—or leading—were powerfully present for me. Like muses asserting themselves into my life, they forced me to take stock: How can I bring my inner and outer life into alignment? What would I do differently if I had no fear of failing? What lesson is my life trying to teach me right now?

These questions are very much alive for me at this writing. They have helped me become clearer about how I am called to lead and what it takes to begin to live my work and life with deeper integrity. Hopefully they will inform my message in fresh and helpful ways. As I reread and rewrite the manuscript in preparation for the updates of this edition, I'm delighted to find two things. One: the earlier concepts still work, but now I understand them in a whole new light of my current experience, sixteen years after the first printing. Two: the questions and new insights that bubbled up out of my personal crisis of integrity have deepened my understanding of leadership and of the leader's most important journey: *the journey inward.*

Faced with new realities, the clients who inspired me to first write this book in 1991 were on a similar journey. They, too, had come to a crisis point in their organizational lives. The old models of leadership—top down, paternalistic, and authoritative—were no longer sufficient. They had embarked on a quest for a new ecology of leadership that was at once tough minded and human; decisive and inclusive. And I joined them in the search. As we perused ideas like servant leadership, values-based management, and personal power, it had become clear to me that beyond the obvious strategic business concerns was a more personal one. The men and women with whom I consulted and collaborated on the subject of leadership wanted more hope, deeper insight, and more honest connection with the humanity in each of us. They wanted to know how to manage self in order to lead change.

This is still the case, as I pen the fourth edition of *Leadership: The Journey Inward.* Then, as now, we continue to experiment with new ways to inspire and mobilize the right kind of leadership needed to reinvent our fledgling and our struggling enterprises. As we reorganize, downsize, and merge formerly competing entities into cautious marriages, we continue to wrestle with penetrating questions of leadership: What will be the effects of our current choices on the next generations? At what point does growing our business become counterproductive? What new strategies and directions must we take to sustain ourselves and our organizations in the new millennium? What new values must guide us in our emerging workplaces? Will we find the courage, the foresight, and the insights necessary to secure our future? How do we develop ourselves to transform our worlds?

Through my work with countless clients in every sector, I remain convinced that the one area of leadership that has been given short shrift is the *inner* work necessary to find our unique "leadership charter." The theme that consistently emerges for me these days is the importance of finding the courage to be ourselves and to exercise leadership from that personal core. I believe that now more than ever, we must attend to our inner lives as we ready ourselves for the leadership challenges before us. I want this edition of *Leadership: The Journey Inward* to speak honestly to the leader in each of us that is calling for personal and organizational renewal amidst the chaos and the promise of our emerging work worlds.

If I am successful, *Leadership: The Journey Inward* will support the battered woman who wants to transform her personal life, as well as the CEO who wants to reinvent the enterprise. If this book serves its purpose, the manager who is faced with yet another restructuring, amidst the wails of shell-shocked displaced workers and disgruntled survivors, will examine different ways to restore individual and organizational well-being. I want to encourage formal leaders to see their role in a new light—to consider "the use of self" as a vehicle for organizational renewal. I will appeal to all of you, regardless of assigned roles, to journey inward and reflect on the hardships and the attendant lessons of your life experience as you attempt to exercise personal and organizational leadership.

At the same time, I am aware of the limits of my personal lens on this subject. I, too, am in process, still walking the path of discovery as I seek to coach others on the subject of leadership. While I am willing to speak passionately about what I know to be true for me, my work has taught me to be cautious of the ready answer. I am learning and teaching the equal importance of living with the right question. So I will raise many questions for you to ponder and to live with, because questions hold the key to self-renewal. And I encourage you to formulate your own questions and to listen carefully for the questions that pop up out of your life experience. For starters, *what question are you living with that prompted you to buy this book?*

As I write this edition of *Leadership: The Journey Inward*, the United States and its allies are at war with Iraq. I am simultaneously unwilling and mesmerized, a "live" participant in a war that technology has brought into my bedroom. I am struck by the paradoxes of leadership and all the unknowns and trepidation around this event and how they mirror the uncertainties of our workplaces. I do not yet know what the outcome will be. But I'm sure that our world will be changed forever.

As new global scenarios unfold, I continue to note lessons from my work and my inner reflections. As part of my personal leadership development practice, I write down my truths, and encourage my clients to create a practice of daily journaling to capture their own truth—the lessons their lives are trying to teach them. I don't assume for a moment that my truth is necessarily the same as yours. I do know that this is a time that calls for serious reflection and that leadership development hinges on our ability to reflect on ourselves and our world. This is in essence why I write. On April 4, 2003, I made the following entry in my Leadership Journal. It surprisingly put me, once again, in touch with my sacred contract—my personal mission as one who encourages self-reflection aimed at personal mastery.

I am witnessing for the first time since I migrated from my native Jamaica to the United States in 1964, the world engaged in real dialogue across spatial and temporal boundaries. Marshall McLuhan's global village is at hand. We are questioning ourselves and each other as international values collide and collapse into each other in some cases. We are living with the paradoxes of dropping bombs and bread simultaneously. Post September 11, 2001, I watched with deep emotion and awe as, for the first time in my memory, a Roman Catholic priest, Jewish rabbi, Muslim imam, and black Baptist minister worshipped together. The words I wrote in 1991 in the opening of Leadership: The Journey Inward *are still true, with the following minor changes: "As global values clash, families re-define, governments re-invent, and businesses re-engineer, our attention rivets on a major concern: do we have the leadership, the vision, the skills, the will, and the resources to secure our future? Will we develop the courage and the wisdom to do the right things on behalf of humanity?"*

This is a book about the courage to exercise leadership in our lives and in our world. It matters very little to me whether the boundaries of your world are drawn around the home in which you practice parent-leadership, or more broadly around the organizations or communities you serve. I want to encourage you to look at the unique ways in which you are called to lead. So we will examine the capacity of ordinary people to exercise leadership in everyday situations, at work or at home, in the community or in personal endeavors.

The first section of the book sets the stage for your **journey inward** to explore how your life experiences and the resulting personal choices may be linked to leadership.

Through self-reflective exercises, you will examine the critical life events that have brought you to wherever you are right now, and the patterns of thought that govern your feelings and actions. This will allow you to discover potential barriers and gateways to your personal development, and identify ways to "let go" and be more open to the risks and choices necessary to unblock your path to more effective leadership.

Our focus will then shift to **the journey outward**. We will explore ways to direct the insights gained through self-reflection to our work with others, in whatever situation we choose. We will explore how you can develop your leadership potential by clarifying your own life purpose, how that purpose fits into your chosen work, your lifestyle, and the groups you belong to.

My hope is that through this book you will create and claim your own leadership path. While I will offer you many examples of how world-renowned leaders emerge and perform, I provide these only because they are people whose leadership stories we may have all heard. These are simply recognizable examples, not recipes for you to follow mechanically. Everyday acts of leadership and followership are based on the same principles as monumental recorded acts of leadership. The goal is for you to find and celebrate your own unique way of leading, while you apply an awareness of the conditions and attributes that others like you have tapped when they chose or were chosen to lead. Keep in mind that whether you are a parent or businessperson, short-order cook or senator, you make leadership choices, or are chosen, based on your life struggles and experiences. By examining those experiences—and the strengths and perspectives each has taught you—you create your own blueprint for continued leadership development with more clarity and confidence.

I will address everyday acts of leadership and review some of the core leadership competencies that will serve us well as we renew our organizations and ourselves. Throughout, I will encourage you to reflect on the soul of leadership. Together we will pursue a deeper understanding of ideas like courage and personal integrity. How can we unleash the hero and heroine in each of us? What would it be like in our families, our workplaces, our communities, and indeed on the planet, if we took the risks necessary to free that part of ourselves that is, in the words of Janet Hagberg, "willing to be other than who the world wants us to be."

As part of the family of humanity, we share a collective consciousness where all of our life stories intersect. With this in mind, I assume that on one level you already know much of what I have to say about the inner journey to find our personal power and our unique leadership edge. On another level influenced by my particular life path and the many teachers whose work I cite throughout the book, I bring yet another lens to the subject. I pray that like the dancing colors of a singular prism that remains the same object, but reveals new aspects of itself with the slightest shifts in perspective, here and there I might shed new light on what we already know.

1 A New Context for Leadership

> *The fact that shadows exist, in the world and in ourselves, should not blind us to the light.... The trouble and pain we inflict and suffer are perfect not in the sense of being "okay," but as an erupting volcano or exploding star is perfect—because such things happen in God's universe.*
>
> —DAN MILLMAN, *Living on Purpose: Straight Answers to Life's Tough Questions*

We are charting new territory. And we have few roadmaps for the emerging landscape in which we must lead, manage, innovate, and serve. Today we make educated guesses as we reinvent our communities and our enterprises, our families and ourselves in a world "flattened" by technological advances, shifting markets, emerging values, and global concerns. Formal leaders now run their organizations by the seat of their pants, merging here, divesting there; staffing up in one instance and downsizing in the next.

Crafting ways to survive and thrive in turbulent times can be tricky business. We aren't always sure about our choices as we cut a passable path to unknown places beyond the horizon. Of course, some are reluctant to let this be known. After all, we are being paid to know what it will take to remain viable and competitive. Savvy management consultants advise executives: "Learn to admit when you don't know. Ask people for their best ideas and listen." But the knowledge that effective leadership hinges on credibility tempts us to pretend to know, even when we don't.

The one thing that is pretty clear to us is this: Change is necessary. The old ways of organizing ourselves and doing business no longer work the way they once did. Old assumptions about lifelong employment, workforce stability, and unconditional loyalty from employees are being challenged. The futurists and trend watchers of the seventies and eighties were right. In the twenty-first century, new paradigms for business, government, community building, and leadership are emerging. Principles of standardization and synchronization that served us well during the Industrial Era are being replaced by new ones. Our workplace stance is shifting from dependence and loyalty to interdependence and employee satisfaction. The focus of our economy has shifted from land and capital to people and information, and from national to global in scope. The extended, rooted, or nuclear family structure has evolved into highly eclectic, flexible arrangements. Attend any wedding or graduation ceremony and the new family structures become apparent. Health policy and health care organizations have shifted from an institutionalized, symptom-driven, reactive stance to the proactive, preventative outlook typified by advocates of wellness and self-care.

These shifts are by no means panaceas for our social problems. They do, however, bring new leadership challenges and countless opportunities with them. In today's climate, **the journey inward** to leadership engages educators, businesspeople, blue-collar workers, the clergy, politicians, professionals, students, and the growing number of unemployed in new ways that may be taxing or exhilarating, depending on the situation and the individual.

Social, environmental, and economic sustainability are the defining concerns of leadership in the twenty-first century. These will require new levels of wisdom and agility from us. Let's take a more detailed look at some sweeping changes in values, educational needs, government, politics, world economics, family, and community that are shaping this new context for leadership.

∞ **The base of our economy has shifted from land development and manufacturing to information technology and services.** As we restructure our organizations and renegotiate our relationships for these new realities, we are moving from top down, paternalistic arrangements to more collaborative ones, from dominator models to alliances. We are also widening our focus from one that is narrow and national to one that is global, socially, environmentally, and economically. The basic premises of our culture's industrial paradigm have been exploded by these shifts. We must now reassess basic assumptions about how we live and lead together.

∞ **Education reform and school-to-work transition have become top priorities for both schools and big business.** About one million young people drop out of U.S. high schools each year. Of the roughly 2.4 million who graduate, 25 percent are functionally illiterate; that is, they are unable to read and write at the eighth-grade level. At the same time, baby boomers are beginning to retire and demographers and trend watchers are predicting a shortage of highly skilled technical workers needed for the "information economy." We see a growing trend towards community grassroots leadership in this and other arenas as educators, unions, businesses, and employees themselves begin to create local, national, and international partnerships for change.

∞ **Employers are shifting their focus: from the cost of paying employees to the value of investing in them; and from workforce stability to workforce resiliency.** No longer do we seek "production-line students" who wait for passive instructions and regurgitate textbook notes. In the Industrial Age, hired hands in jobs were sufficient. Today employers try to engage the hearts and minds of workers as well. We must find ways to inspire renewed loyalty, trust, and commitment from the existing workforce as we recruit and develop a new pool of employees that can pose new questions and challenge the status quo. This is crucial if we are to craft more stable, resilient, high performing enterprises.

∞ **Employees, likewise, are changing their expectations.** Lifestyle integration into work life is driving movements like family-friendly work practices. Job sharing, flextime, and cafeteria-style benefits packages that are individualized to employee needs are now commonplace. So are concierge services where employees can access perks from babysitting to dry cleaning with the support of their employers. In the emerging leadership environment, employees are both uncertain that they can trust employers to make good on the assumed promise of job security and more assertive about their needs. A steady job and making a living are still important concerns. But so are a growing desire for meaningful work and a life that works.

∞ **Product and service quality continue to shape a new course for industry, government and schools.** We can no longer rely solely on marketing and price differentiation to meet competition. Customers are more fickle and better able to exercise the right to choose, and developments like the World Wide Web are revolutionizing supplier/customer relationships, transforming service and our economy in dramatic ways.

∞ **Americans work longer hours today than they did twenty years ago.** Despite complaints from workplace veterans that "the old work ethic is dying," research shows that the average American worker puts in forty-nine hours per week, a 20 percent increase over 1970 figures. This may be partly due to the rise in small-business owners who tend to work longer hours. It is also somewhat attributable to what has been called the "baby-boomer work ethic," associated with the stereotypical driven, successful Wall Street yuppies of the '80s. At the same time, Generation Xers, who in their thirties are moving into leadership roles, bring refreshing new perspectives that will reshape this trend even as I write. Their grandparents' mantra was "Take care of me, and I will be unconditionally loyal." In contrast, the Generation Xers' loyalty is conditional: "Show me you care, and I will give you my best work." This generation, the "latchkey kids" of the seventies, are leading the way to more family-friendly practices.

∞ **Each year, six hundred thousand immigrants enter the United States legally, in addition to an estimated one million illegal immigrants.** The impact of immigration on our nation creates a series of domestic issues that affect education, business, and the overall community. How the leaders in various sectors choose to handle immigration policies will have a major impact on the size and make-up of the United States over the next decade. We know that the increased interactions cross-culturally aided by immigration and travel patterns will grow and stretch us in beneficial ways. We are also aware of the need for new leadership skills to facilitate cultural inclusivity.

∞ **Diversity has emerged as one of the most critical issues in the twenty-first century workplace.** We have come to realize that our lack of sensitivity and skill in dealing with differences will have serious organizational consequences unless we learn to value and manage diversity. We now understand that the most competitive corporate leaders will be those who create a work environment where people can bring the very best they have to offer—regardless of their family status, job classification, gender, race, age, creed, sexual orientation, physical attributes or abilities, socioeconomic status, or country of birth.

∞ **Many employees, especially women and minorities, formerly preoccupied with breaking through the "corporate glass ceiling" now voluntarily leave to take on entrepreneurial ventures.** Or, where economically feasible, some have traded in their business suits to focus on child rearing, sparking a reverse movement from office to home. And this is not the only group moving in that direction. Technology has made it possible for thousands of men and women to telecommute from home. This reflects a new worker mindset. Some people have become more autonomous in their outlook. They no longer feel they have to have their needs met in the traditional workplace.

∞ **Family issues are redefining our political, social, and economic agenda,** as we address new crises

connected with health care, elder care, teen pregnan-
cies, youth crime, school safety, and early childhood
education.

∞ **In some parts of the United States, prisons are being touted as the new growth industry.** A high-tech
prison near Oregon, for example, housed 4,000 inmates
following a facility expansion. The community leaders
were pleased that this change caused the community's
population (which lay dormant for many years) to rise
by more than 15 percent because the prison created 500
new jobs.

Add to the above sampling of trends increased environmental awareness, questions of global sustainability, advances in science and technology, and we get a rough picture of the incredible leadership challenges facing those
who embark on the leadership journey.

These developments, for better or for worse, are the
legacy of past choices. We have reaped many benefits from
our wise choices. There is more than enough progress in areas like technology and medicine to show for our past efforts.
We have profited greatly worldwide from effective management and the wise leadership of many of our endeavors.

But the costs of progress have also been high. Today's
environment, economy, and our children are paying the
price for our past mistakes. There have been leaders in every sector who have sacrificed long-term effectiveness for
short-term wins. Current organizational efforts aimed at
quality, work process redesign, mergers, downsizing,
school reform, reinventing government, multinational partnerships, multicultural sensitivity, work/family balance, and
environmental protection acknowledge our errors of the

past and our concerns for the future. We are being called to make amends for mistakes like slavery, apartheid, the disruption of biodiversity, and corporate greed. As we move into an age of endless personal and global dilemmas, we must become even more creative architects of an uncertain future.

Most enterprise executives now recognize that the best laid managerial plans will fail if they are not guided by leaders who have the character and skills to *reestablish trust and enable people* to execute the plans. Managerial and technical training are still important to ensure well-run organizations, but my clients in business, government, and the not-for-profit sector have become more concerned with how to educate and develop *a new breed of leaders* at all organizational levels.

Redefining Leadership for the New Realities

Scholarly attempts to define leadership have varied widely. It is very much like the definition of the elephant as perceived by the blind men in Aesop's fable. Each described the part of the animal that he stood near and could touch. One described the shape and size of the tail, another a leg, and so on; all different but true. Combine the descriptions, and they make up the whole animal. Likewise, the concept of leadership has evolved over time from the "single great man" theory, to personal traits theories, to situational and style-based models.

The trends outlined in this chapter represent yet another conceptualization of leadership: *shared leadership.* Vertical (top down) approaches are now being complemented by horizontal ones. We are forming strategic alliances with former competitors and across former departmental and global divides. The sharing of resources across our differences calls for a new kind of leadership rooted in trust, flexibility, and open communications.

We are also more mindful than ever of the values that underpin our leadership efforts. Consider the titles of the following popular books on the new leadership paradigms: *The Heart Aroused: Poetry and the Preservations of the Soul in Corporate America, Encouraging the Heart: A Leader's Guide to Rewarding and Recognizing Others, Leadership and Spirit: Breathing New Vitality and Energy Into Individuals and Organizations.* These authors are affirming a new direction in our conceptualization of leadership—the belief that to be truly effective at transforming others, we must first transform ourselves. We are now, more than ever, preoccupied with questions like: What values and character traits inform our leadership choices? To what extent can we demonstrate trustworthiness in our leadership—a show of competence, integrity, and goodwill? How can we become good corporate citizens who balance concern for economic gain with concern for humanity?

In fact, many social scientists now claim that our planet's very survival may depend on our ability to produce a new breed of highly ethical, participative leaders at all levels: from the loftiest reaches of business and government to grassroots community organizations and families. This awareness may well account for our present preoccupation with public scrutiny of those who choose to lead, be they CEO or politician, evangelist or parent.

Clearly, we must shift our position from a focus on short-term goals to long-term thinking; from maintaining today's status quo to creating the future we desire; from depending on institutions to self-reliance; from competition to partnerships. This book was written to help you prepare for these new leadership challenges. It is designed as a self-study course that will allow you to draw on your own life experiences to develop your capacity to exercise leadership in different areas of your life, in different situations. The concepts and exercises presented target a range of enterprises and institutions. They apply equally to public sector and private sector concerns. They should be useful to technical specialists, professionals, and operatives at any level, and helpful whether or not you are engaged in official acts of "managing" or "leading."

2 How Leaders Emerge

The point is not to become a leader. The point is to become yourself, to use yourself completely—all your skills, gifts and energies—in order to make your vision manifest.

—WARREN BENNIS *and*
BURT NANUS, *Leaders*

Put a group of people together in a room. Give them a task to do, and leadership happens. One or more persons in the group will answer an inner or outer call to *influence* the group. Through a series of thoughts and actions, the emergent leader gets self and others to move in a particular way, in a particular direction. If successful, he or she facilitates a *desired* outcome for all concerned. This is the most basic definition of leadership: *the capacity to achieve the outcomes we want.* I call it leadership whether it occurs in the corridors of our enterprises, in the battlefields of humanity, between a parent and child, or inside ourselves as we pursue personal mastery. And I see it as a natural and necessary part of human interaction and survival.

Managing versus Leading

It may be helpful at this point to make a distinction between "managing" and "leading," for there is a place for both, and the effective manager or leader must recognize when to use each. Management aims at **maintenance**. When we don our management hat, we want to make sure that organizational goals are met efficiently and profitably, with a minimal amount of disruption. The same applies in personal or family life. When we manage our lives effectively, we are on top of the day-to-day demands.

Leadership, by contrast, aims at **change**. When we step into this role our goal is to inspire and empower others to respond to challenges by using their creativity to secure the best possible future for all concerned. Similarly, when we exercise leadership in our personal lives, we work through crises creatively and push ourselves and perhaps others to new levels of effectiveness.

Of course this distinction between managing and leading is somewhat artificial. Show me a good "manager," and I will show you someone who has good leadership skills as described in this book. Conversely, show me a good "leader"—one with visionary ideas, passion, and an ability to influence change—and I will show you someone who also knows how to manage those ideals into implementation or who surrounds him- or herself with the right people to get the job done.

In times of crisis and transformation such as we now face, we need both formal and informal leaders—people who believe, who inspire performance, who are credible and persuasive enough to get people and things moving in the best direction. And we need different kinds of leaders, again both formal and informal. We need idea leaders: activists who will put their beliefs and viewpoints and sometimes even their lives on the line. We need servant leaders who appear whenever help is needed. We need enterprise leaders, and community leaders, and spiritual leaders, and those who lead by simply showing up and exuding intangibles like love and goodness, who model a way of life that warms our hearts and inspires us to look more deeply into our souls. Each type of leadership has its own contribution to make to humanity, each its own special quality. We need leadership in all these forms and more, and from situation to situation. As we alternate between our roles as followers and leaders, we can all benefit from a healthy mix of these leadership stances within ourselves as well.

Leadership is what humans do, in varying degrees, as we wrestle with the events of our personal and work lives. It is at once a *process*, a collection of *behaviors*, and a *stance* we take as we seek to achieve the outcomes we want and prevent those we don't want. If you trace the etymology of the word *lead* it takes you back to the basic intent of leadership: to cause to go along one's way. This is true whether we are dealing with the will of the individual leader, or the will of the collective. In the end, *leadership is very simply about influence and goal attainment.*

There is nothing inherently noble about leadership, although noble acts are sometimes achieved through leadership. But leadership, per se, is no more or less sacred than "followership." Because leadership is often called for in the face of crisis and uncertainty, it is given more play in our studies and in our workplaces. In some respects, this has been to our detriment. For example, to get really well rewarded for our hard work, we must be promoted into the ranks of managerial or professional "leadership," not followership. Yet, in the course of followership, carrying out the mandates of our supervisors or completing the mundane tasks required of our discipline, people routinely commit everyday acts of leadership—they choose to influence others towards a goal. These acts often go unacknowledged and unrewarded, but they are acts of leadership nonetheless.

If you observe people who set out to make things happen, you will notice predictable behaviors that are relatively easy to document. They may nudge, cajole, innovate, coach, dictate, inspire, or try to persuade in other ways. They may rely on charisma, integrity, or force of will. They may call into play their organizational clout or their inner resources. When behavioral scientists observe group dynamics, they might use terms like counterdependent, interdependent, or independent to label the emergent leader, depending on the stance he or she takes. They might make note of whether the leader's approach tends to be more task oriented or people oriented. Then, depending on the leadership theories they subscribe to, they might further designate the leadership style along a continuum from autocratic on one extreme to laissez faire on the other. It is safe to conclude that regardless of how feats of leadership are accomplished, they tend to rely on similar types of observable behaviors.

When I observe people with an eye to developing organizational leaders, I make note of the leadership competencies and character traits that were called into play as the leader (or co-leaders) attempted to influence others to achieve the desired end state. Did the observed leader challenge the status quo and offer up some vision of an attractive outcome? Did he or she formulate an effective strategy? Was the leader able to maintain credibility, build morale, resolve conflict, and create a climate that supports creativity, problem solving, and "right" decisions? Did the leader value diversity and inclusivity so that each group member had ample opportunity to make a full contribution? These are all valid and useful pieces of the study of leadership.

There still remains the largely unanswered question of how leadership develops in the first place, and what "ordinary" people can do to hone their leadership skills. Why, for example, do some people choose to lead while others follow—or still others do neither? Does one have to be a great person to be considered a leader? If so, what is the source of this "greatness"? Is it innate or inborn? Is it inspired by parents or mentors? Is it a function of intelligence, or is it mere grit?

Early in my career, in an attempt to learn as much about leadership as I could, I read about those whose leadership successes were well documented. My students and I studied the lives of exemplary leaders like Gandhi, Mother Teresa, John F. Kennedy, Marcus Garvey, Winston Churchill, Golda Meir, Florence Nightingale, Martin Luther King, Jr., Moses, and Einstein. We were surely looking in the right places to find the great lessons of leadership. But we often used limited lenses, focusing on notables from the distant past and too narrowly on questions about their leadership approaches. We explored the shared characteristics of great leaders, the reasons for their successes, what attracted followers to them, and most important, how to emulate them or learn from them as we studied how to become effective leaders. These questions were, and still are, important to ask. They gave us many valuable insights into leadership. However, the most critical insight was not what I expected.

We make the world lonelier and less interesting by yearning for heroes. We deny the constant, inclusionary creating that is going on; we deny our own capacity to contribute and expand.

—MARGARET J. WHEATLEY
and MYRON KENNER-ROGERS

It is quite simply this: there are few, if any, universal paths to leadership. Sometimes leadership emerges from the ranks of nobility; at other times, it emerges from the squalor of poverty. Some leaders were reared by parents who inspired and supported them to do and be their best. Others had their resolve to lead shaped by abusive parents. My work with leadership has confirmed this. I meet leaders who emerge at every level in organizations, and who come from all walks of life. I also meet people who hold positions of high status who are not exercising leadership. At the same time, being an operative at the lowest rung of the organizational ladder does not necessarily prevent one from exercising leadership, where appropriate. While there is still an important role for formal leaders who create and manage organizations, smart executives include all members in a shared leadership process, where everyone's talents and perspectives are deployed to deliver quality goods and services.

When an ordinary person exercises extraordinary leadership—inspiring others to do or be more, changing the course of events in small communities, or in history—it is usually because of one or both of the following reasons:

1. The individual has made a fundamentally personal choice to influence his or her situation. For some, this is a decision to act with integrity: to do the right thing in order to make a difficult situation better. For others, the motive may be much more self-serving; they may want to be seen as powerful or effective in the world. In either case, if followers are attracted to the leader's vision, the person who chooses to lead has an impact.

2. Followers choose the leader. They notice something he or she is doing, or they perceive attributes of the

would-be leader that they find attractive. They then decide to either follow the individual's lead, or press that person into leadership. As one writer on leadership put it, if you look over your shoulder and people are following, you are a leader.

Rosa Parks exercised leadership when she decided, weary and worn out, to do the right thing on a bus in Montgomery, Alabama on her way home from work one evening. The management team of Johnson & Johnson exercised leadership when, in the aftermath of the Tylenol scare, they chose to do the right thing: be honest with the media and public and directly confront the problem of their tainted, over-the-counter medication. (In the end, they gained customers due to their integrity.)

There are countless other examples every day: Jennifer Daniels, a teenage mother of two, exercised leadership when, after putting herself through college at night, she decided to spend her time counseling and encouraging other teen parents to pursue their dreams; Mahatma Gandhi decided to stand up against the social injustices that blocked his path to career success; Samuel Gordon, an eighth-grade dropout, took on two jobs to move his family to a safer neighborhood and put each of his six children through college; Benazir Bhutto, in her moment of personal crisis, decided to continue her father's work and adopt his political responsibilities in a culture where few, if any, women possess such power; Dr. Sandra Murray, a leading African American scientist, nurtured an interest in anatomy and cell biology that took her from the South Side of Chicago to international prominence in her field; and Mikhail Gorbachev and Ronald Reagan decided to take a different approach, ending the Cold War. Some of these people's leadership actions have been duly noted in the pages of history. Others will never be written about, except in this brief paragraph. All have one thing in common:

These ordinary human beings chose to have an extraordinary impact on the situations in which they found themselves. In the words of Eleanor Roosevelt, they decided it was "better to light a candle than to curse the darkness."

As I discuss in subsequent chapters, there are also vast differences in the styles of leaders. Some are shy and retiring, not given to oratorical brilliance or political maneuvering, while others thrive on these qualities. Some attract followers by listening and responding, others by vehement, forceful persuasion. In fact, I have come to believe that there are as many leadership paths as there are leaders!

In the end, the common thread that binds all leaders is that their emergence into leadership came about as they tried to resolve personal life crises or dilemmas of choice in their organizations or communities. Each of the leaders cited thus far was trying to make sense of his or her world, and in the process engaged others in trying to change the world. Each could just as easily have chosen to succumb to the challenges life presented them, but chose instead to exercise personal and/or organizational power.

Leadership begins and ends with the internal developmental struggles of the individual leader. It is by integrating and learning from these crises that we gain the stamina and tools of effective leadership. In short, our blueprint for leadership is imbedded in our own life story. Winston Churchill understood this well when, upon being called into leadership of the British war effort, he commented, "All of my life experiences have prepared me for this hour."

We all embody leadership potential. That is, each of us is capable of influencing people and situations. Choosing to exercise this potential or demonstrating effective leadership behaviors varies by the individual and the circumstances he or she faces. Often, our decision to lead arises out of a personal crisis. In the process of figuring out how to cope with crises, we may strengthen our leadership qualities and use these merits to creatively solve these situations and move forward. In the process of this resolution, we sometimes engage others, thereby exercising "leadership."

At times we are pressed into leadership by others—our children, our employers, our communities. These "followers" may call forth our talents because they admire the stand we have taken or qualities we exhibit. Or they may simply decide to emulate the actions we take as we successfully wrestle with challenges. The would-be leader ultimately makes the personal choice to rise to the occasion. Folklore has it that Martin Luther King, Jr. did not explicitly set out to lead the civil rights movement. Circumstances called forth his leadership when he was selected by followers who decided that his gifts of eloquence, his philosophy, and his impact on others were needed to address the racial crises of the moment.

The following are examples of the evolution of leadership out of personal struggles. In some cases, I have selected people who became famous, and therefore known to most readers. I have also included examples from lesser-known people as a reminder that we all embody the capacity to lead. Like each of us, these leaders were faced with resolving personal needs and made choices from dramatic activist stances on one extreme to decisions to adopt new stances in their personal lives. As you read these accounts, I invite you to reflect on times when you experienced injustice or felt strongly about changing a situation.

Rosa Parks, who is regarded by many as an important civil rights leader, epitomizes the meaning of this book. What Mrs. Parks did, quite simply, was to decide—in a moment of personal crisis—that she had reached the end of her rope! Her decision to empower herself, to finally do the right thing in a situation she had endured for countless years, underscores the nature of leadership as an act of courage.

Tired from a long day's work and from years of racial discrimination that forced her to live with the daily humiliation of having to give up her seat to whites, she finally confronted her moment of crisis, leaned in, and emerged a leader. Hers is a dramatic example of how a seemingly insignificant woman ignited an entire movement by a single act of personal power. She described her actions and feelings in a recent interview compiled by Brian Lanker:

> *When he saw that I was still remaining in the seat, the driver said,*
>
> *"If you don't stand up, I'm going to call the police and have you arrested." I said, "You may do that."*
>
> *Two policemen came and wanted to know what was the trouble.*
>
> *One said, "Why don't you stand up?" I said, "I don't think I should have to." At that point I asked the policeman, "Why do you push us around?" He said, "I don't know, but the law is the law and you're under arrest."*

Mrs. Parks then went on to offer an interesting account of leadership by example, and the relationship of followership, leadership, and personal power:

People just stayed off the buses because I was arrested, not because I asked them [to]. If everybody else had been happy and doing well, my arrest wouldn't have made any difference at all . . . there was a kind of lifting of a burden from me individually. I could feel that whatever my individual desires were to be free, I was not alone. . . . Many whites, even white Southerners, told me that even though it may have seemed like the blacks were being freed (by my actions), they felt more free and at ease themselves. They thought that my action didn't just free blacks, but them too.

This account, and the ones that follow, highlight three important observations about the emergence of leadership:

1. **You do not have to willfully set out to "be a leader" in order to exercise leadership.** If you demonstrate courage, honesty, integrity, and conviction in the way you go about resolving personal and interpersonal crises, you will sometimes emerge as a leader if people find your actions engaging.

2. **Followers empower leaders to lead.** It is the followers' perception that ultimately determines the scope of the leader's influence.

3. **When confronted with choice points in our lives, the direction we choose for ourselves will determine whether we exercise leadership—creating the future we desire—or succumb to the pressure.** Also, whether we choose to lead or succumb depends on a variety of factors such as the circumstance, the people involved, our state of mind, our prior experiences and level of expertise, and our needs and motivations at the moment of choice.

Lech Walesa outwardly demonstrated his personal resolve when he scaled a 12-foot-high wall into the Lenin shipyard to start the first of his now famous sit-ins on behalf of the Solidarity Labor Union members. Again, his struggle was, at its core, a personal one. Lech Walesa was the first to admit that he was chosen by his followers. In his words, "In Poland, everyone is a leader." But his personal indignation and his vision of new possibility fueled his ability to exert great influence towards creating a free Poland.

Corazon Aquino, a well-educated woman, was reportedly very content with her role of mother and statesman's devoted wife. She had no personal aspirations for the presidency of the Philippines. However, in wrestling with her personal life crisis—how to resolve the assassination of her husband—she reached inward, tapping her courage and the lessons her life experiences had taught her over the years. In a critical moment, she decided that the path she must take; the right thing to do under the circumstances was to carry forward her husband's work by becoming president of the Philippines.

Empowered by willing followers, she tapped into her leadership potential, translating personal crisis into decisive action. Similar stories can be told of Coretta Scott King, who carried on the work of Martin Luther King, Jr.; or Myrlie Evers-Williams, widow of slain civil rights leader Medgar Evers, who was elected as the first woman to chair the NAACP.

Mahatma Gandhi, a shy humanist in his early life, was also propelled into exemplary leadership by his decisions following a critical turning point.

While en route to South Africa by train, he was denied access to a stagecoach because of his race. He was so enraged by this injustice that, in the words of B. R. Nanda, his biographer, "the iron entered his soul." At that point, he **resolved to change his world** by devoting his life to stamping out injustice.

To make the point of this chapter, I have chosen somewhat dramatic examples in which personal indignation or even rage may play a part in the individual's emergence into leadership. The simple lesson here is that leadership is tied to **conviction**. Leaders have a vision of a better future; they feel strongly about positively influencing the future. They reach inward and tap into their storehouse of experiences to empower, inspire, influence, and collaborate with others to successfully meet the future's challenges. A sense of purpose drives leaders; their actions are future oriented and hopeful.

For some leaders, the moment of crisis that propels them forward is distinct and dramatic. For others, like Margaret Thatcher, it is a steady evolution in which the leader is groomed for success from birth. Thatcher was raised in a family active in community affairs, consumed with politics, religion, and the work ethic. Heavily influenced by her upbringing, Thatcher, upon entering Oxford University, immediately joined the Oxford University Conservative Association as a Tory. She became president of the Association in her senior year, and decided to pursue a career in politics upon graduation. By age 26, Thatcher won the Tory nomination representing the district of Dartford. This was quite a significant achievement at the time, especially since she was a "first": a young woman who defeated 26 other candidates, all male, for the political seat.

Thatcher's subsequent campaigns for political office were not all rosy. She was defeated twice in her attempt to be elected to Parliament. But her highly disciplined upbringing served her well. She campaigned with vigor, working day and night, and through this and other grueling ordeals, eventually earned the nickname "The Iron Lady." Her political career was firmly launched in 1959, when she won a seat in the House of Commons. By then she had married, attended law school, and passed the bar exams (while five months pregnant with twins). While carrying out the traditional roles of wife, mother, and homemaker, she maintained her career with unrelenting vigor.

Margaret Thatcher's rise to Prime Minister of England in 1979 marked the culmination of years of struggle by a woman who was **groomed to succeed** by parental nurturing, academic and professional mentors, as well as the political climate in her country—in short, a total environment that called forth this woman's **innate leadership potential**.

It is easy to find documented examples of the lives and struggles of political, social, scientific, and artistic leaders and their journeys toward excellence. Other notables whose personal paths to leadership have been well documented include various members of the Kennedy family, General George Patton, educator Marva Collins, Winston Churchill, Golda Meir, Booker T. Washington, Mary McLeod Bethune, Albert Einstein, Madame Marie Curie, Leonard Bernstein, Vincent Van Gogh, Pablo Picasso, and Paul Robeson, to name a few.

Only recently have we begun to document the lives of business people as the new "heroes." We now relish biographies and autobiographies of people like Bill Gates, H. Ross Perot, Lee Iacocca, Mary Kay Ash, Jack Welsh, as well as "rebel employees turned leaders." Erin Brockovich is now a household name in American lore. Here is a rank-and-file worker in a lowly administrative post, answering phone calls in a law firm. She uses her only power source—inner conviction and personal courage—to change the course of events. Similar stories of so-called Enron whistle-blower Sherron Watkins, are being told everywhere. Even though she never technically blew a whistle, she is hailed as a trail-blazer by the masses who admire her gumption for her cautionary note to her boss. According to *Time Magazine,* she wrote a cryptic missive warning her boss, "I am incredibly nervous that we will implode in a wave of accounting scandals." That single decision to speak her truth, that personal choice to frame her world as she saw it made her a beacon for leadership when her letter unwittingly fell into the hands of the media and on the ears of the multitudes. Watkins and others now routinely make the media rounds and bestseller lists, providing us with inspiring examples of the inner journey of those who choose to make their impact in business and industry.

These people did not necessarily make their start in life out of greatness. Lee Iacocca, for example, admits to being an extremely shy person who balked at public presentations. In struggling with this personal challenge, he sought out Dale Carnegie courses and pushed himself to take on more and more challenging speaking engagements to improve his effectiveness. While I would not venture to attribute all of his corporate success to this single life crisis, his eventual mastery of media communications exemplifies the link between developmental struggles and resolving to lead.

If you look around your own workplace, you will doubtless find similar examples that will never come to the attention of the media, but are still examples of useful acts of leadership. A Pittsburgh Paint and Glass (PPG) scientist I know demonstrated this kind of leadership when he saw an opportunity to turn waste into a viable product. He observed that the company's paint manufacturing customers generated a waste product that was expensive to dispose of. It occurred to the scientist that this waste could be reprocessed and sold as a low-grade paint to be applied to such products as industrial drums that did not require expensive applications. This technical research professional showed leadership as he championed this idea through all the proper internal channels. The customer now pays PPG less than it would have to dispose of the product, for the service of retrieving and recycling the paint. The customer, and others, can then purchase the paint for other uses. In this clever, innovative move, everyone wins. By empowering a technical staff member, who is typically not charged with taking the company into new markets, PPG has created a motivating environment that supports the emergence of leadership in its employees.

Oprah Winfrey, has been an inspiring example of someone who uses her media presence as a powerful platform for personal leadership. As she shares accounts of her humble beginnings and her struggles with child sexual abuse and the like, she exemplifies the "use of self" as a motivating force as she encourages her listeners to be more effective in their own lives.

Finally, like the Rosa Parks story, there continue to be extraordinary events that call forth or highlight our leadership prowess when we least expect it. Browsing through my neighborhood bookstore, the title of a new book jumped out at me. Not surprisingly for me, it said "LEADERSHIP" in bold reddish brown letters. I slid the book off the shelf curious to read what yet another fellow writer has to add to our understanding of this much-perused subject. Underneath the title is the stately photograph of the man who epitomizes leadership for this book. The large white letters across the book's lower edge reads "Rudolph W. Guiliani."

He is both the author and the subject of this book on leadership. As fate, and followers would have it, Guiliani emerged as a name synonymous with leadership because of one awful event in time. When *Time Magazine* dubbed him Person of the Year, the inscription said it all:

> *For having more faith in us than we had in ourselves, for being brave when required and rude where appropriate and tender without being trite, for not sleeping and not quitting and not shrinking from the pain all around him, Rudy Guiliani, Mayor of the World.*

Once again, we are reminded that leadership is often born of crisis.

3 Self-Knowledge: Prerequisite for Leadership

For what will it profit you if you gain the whole world,

but lose your soul?

—JESUS OF NAZARETH

As I sit in my window tapping out an earlier edition of *Leadership: The Journey Inward* on my keyboard, I get a pop-up e-mail message on the computer screen. It's from a current client, a project leader at a Fortune 100 company. "Thanks," it reads, "for what you do to help heal our workplace. I am beginning to understand the connection between who I am and how I lead." I lean over, print the message, and slip it into a file I keep on my desk, labeled "Blessings from My Work." I return to my writing, filled with gratitude for the opportunity to serve through my own small everyday acts of personal leadership. The practice of acknowledging the spiritual rewards of my work is important me.

Reflecting now on the e-mail message, I am struck by this manager's tone. It is such a departure from the stance executives invariably took two decades ago when I started this work. The man who penned this e-mail works in an industry where hard-nosed competition, rigorous analysis, and tough decision making are the touchstones of success. He is good at these things and will continue to be. Yet he sought me out after hearing me speak at a leadership conference because he felt off balance. "I liked your reference to Zora Neale Hurston," he said, and went on to explain how, like Hurston, the contents of his "inner self" had shifted. He, too, was exercising outer leadership in his work world while living with a crisis of integrity internally, where has inner and outer worlds were not in alignment. His workplace victories were beginning to feel hollow. He was struggling to find something deeper, but wasn't sure what it was. As we worked together, he came to realize that his was a call to connect in more meaningful ways with his current work, rather than to follow his initial impulse to leave his company altogether. He was living with a definition of success that was self-limiting, and has since learned to redefine success in broader, more liberating terms.

A basic premise of this book is that even the greatest, most enabling leader is at the core an "ordinary person," with ordinary fears, concerns, and life challenges. I take the somewhat irreverent position that all of us embody the potential to lead. Some of us tap this potential and use it to positively influence the situations in which we find ourselves. Others succumb to life pressures or are never challenged to exercise leadership. Still others harness it, but use it for self-serving or malevolent ends.

One thing is clear if we choose to lead: **To transform our organizations, our communities, or our lives, we must first transform ourselves.** Leadership development, is a process of self-reflection aimed at personal growth: a journey inward.

Organizational renewal must begin with personal renewal because organizations do not exist as entities apart from the people that compose them. *In fact, we recreate ourselves through our organizations.* If we are personally lacking in integrity, low in self-esteem, or careless about our environment, then the organizations we create as leaders will mirror our lack of values, our insecurities, or our carelessness. To create organizations or communities that are responsive and responsible, we must first make sure that we are ourselves capable of making the right decisions and acting with courage and responsibility.

Once we regularly engage in self-reflection, it becomes easier to be in touch with the significance of the challenges and the opportunities that present themselves in our personal and professional lives. We can then consciously draw on and apply these lessons to the development of a personal plan for our own leadership development.

When we are self-reflective and willing to explore the lessons behind life crises, we tend to keep moving towards greater personal power and influence. This means confronting each challenge, taking the attendant risks, and developing new competencies as a result. Wisdom comes from our ability to reflect on ourselves honestly and our willingness to invest ourselves in the pain and profits of risk-taking and self-knowledge. This is often challenging. At times it evokes deep-seated fears because it requires that we lean into uncomfortable situations and confront unloved parts of ourselves. It also requires a willingness to take risks and work through difficulties in order to learn what possible outcomes and information about ourselves lurk behind the wall. But for those who would make an impact on their world, it is a path worth taking. In the words of Marilyn Ferguson, author of *The Aquarian Conspiracy*:

> *Risk always brings its own rewards: the exhilaration of breaking through, of getting to the other side; the relief of a conflict healed; the clarity when a paradox dissolves. Whoever teaches us, this is the agent of*

our liberation. Eventually we know deeply that the other side of every fear is freedom.

In her landmark book, *Real Power: Stages of Personal Power in Organizations,* Janet Hagberg speaks eloquently about "The Wall," a place of transformation on our personal and leadership journey. She describes it as a place of simultaneous loss and gain—a place that is at once exhilarating and painful. In her words:

> *The wall is the place we face our inner selves, the truth of who we are, our shame, and ultimately our heart's deepest desires. We embrace all of this and learn to accept it. People describe the process of moving through the wall in these other ways; as a deep well, an abyss, a slow descent, a dark tunnel, a pit, a prison cell, a dark night. It is never pretty. But in it are glimpses of wisdom and light. And it is healing, at a deep level, a soul level.*

We come to the wall because things no longer make sense the way they were. Old definitions of success, for example, no longer work for us when we think of what is meaningful in our work. We come to the wall because we desire more depth in our lives or because we have experienced a loss, as is the case with many of my clients who suddenly face downsizing or an illness in midlife. We come to the wall because our soul beckons us to answer a call to more authenticity in our lives; because we can no longer hide from ourselves.

At this wall we are called to embark on a journey inward. We are invited to engage in a process of self-renewal through self-knowledge. We are given the opportunity to gather up the lessons our life is trying to teach us—to mine our gems of wisdom, to heal our work lives and to lead with a clearer sense of purpose and integrity.

Unfortunately it is possible to get stuck and never be able to transcend this stage of personal development. When this happens, we may put our energy into denying the significance of our lives and the challenges and lessons life presents. When we are "stuck," we may avoid struggle or succumb to it. We look for the easy way out, drowning our confusion in more work or other excesses. In the end, the very consequence we fear, such as loss of control or lack of power, becomes our reality. As a result, we are less likely to exercise personal power or have a deeper, more meaningful experience of leadership. Nor are we likely to change our worlds in positive ways. Those who continue to lead from this stuck place, devoid of self-knowledge and integrity, are more likely to become tyrannical leaders. Possessed by fear, insecurity, and egomania, we may fall into the trap of leading by coercion or inspiring terror in others.

What I'm betting on is this. If we journey inward with good intentions, we will connect with the Goodness in ourselves. If we honestly examine our shadow sides—the unloved parts of ourselves that oppose the best in us—and come to accept our limitations, frailties, and habits that harm self and others, we free ourselves to unleash the best we have to offer. Then we can more honestly and passionately mobilize our strengths, talents, wisdom, and the humanity in each of us that wants to serve. The trick lies in leaving ourselves **open** to lessons our lives attempt to teach us. Only then will we clarify our values and determine what is important and what is insignificant at work, at home, and in our communities.

In the section that follows, I provide a simple process that I use with clients in my Journey Inward Retreats. This "life mapping" exercise allows participants to identify life patterns—both ineffective and effective—by charting critical life events, key people, personal choices, their impact on the individual, and the lessons learned. By becoming aware of your patterns, you can redirect your energy and create more positive outcomes for yourself. You can do this in two ways:

1. You can identify patterns that block your success, then "reprogram" these negative patterns by consciously changing your thinking and the behaviors your thinking supports.

2. You can identify patterns that have created your successes, then consciously reinforce and build upon the thinking and behaviors that support these patterns.

Life Mapping: Taking the Journey Inward

To begin with, let's consider this: No two people are the same. Even identical twins have different footprints and unique elements of spirit. Similarly, each of us is given a life script that is ours alone. We each have a special combination of strengths and weaknesses, trials and successes that are like no other.

Over a lifetime our unique journey unfolds as a series of stories told to us by the events and people we encounter and by the results of the choices we make along the way. Each story brings a special message. Each holds a lesson to be learned as we develop wisdom and strategies to create the outcomes we seek and prevent those we don't want. Often we ignore these lessons. As a result, we repeat them over and over until we become enlightened. As you complete the Life Mapping exercise that follows, you may notice certain recurring themes or patterns. For example, you may find that each time you are on the verge of financial success something occurs to set you back. Or you may find that you are attracted, over and over again, to a certain kind of relationship that starts in a particular way and ends in a particular way.

As you practice self-reflection, you will get to know your patterns more intimately. Because the most direct route to personal development is an ability to reflect on our lives and the lessons our experiences have taught us, you will gain greater clarity about how your personal patterns inform the ways to lead, follow, and live your life. By taking stock of our strengths, weaknesses and inclinations, we can redirect our energies for more effective personal and organizational results.

We are all reared in cultures and families that teach their myths—stories with a deeper allegorical meaning—that offer codes for living. From our earliest bedtime stories to the legendary family recollections that are repeated over and over at holiday gatherings; from the wise teachings of spiritual leaders and elders to the rumblings of the company grapevines, these stories are rich with information for our survival. Each offers up metaphors or themes to help us remember what is true, what is sacred, what is important. When I contract with an organization to conduct a culture audit, I start by getting all members of the enterprise to share their stories. This allows me to help my clients quickly decode aspects of themselves and their work culture that are hidden from everyday awareness. So view this process as a storytelling exercise in which the myths and metaphors of your own life become clearer in the telling of your stories.

To get us started, I offer this excerpt from my own child-hood recollection as an example:

At the very early age of three, I was given a minor role in a concert at the elementary school where my mother taught. I was to mount the seemingly vast stage and recite a poem that went simply: "Look, there's a spider on the wall. That's all!"

Filled with anticipation, I was hoisted up on to the stage by my mother, and in what was to become my earliest recollection of consciousness, I thought: "I don't see a spider. I won't say those words!" So I stood there transfixed, saying nothing as all the teachers sitting in the front row of the auditorium whispered in increasingly nervous tones, "Go ahead, honey, say the poem. Go ahead . . . 'Look there's a spider . . .' Go ahead. Don't be scared!"

To which I finally replied defiantly: "I won't say it. There is no spider on the wall!"

So they put the concert on hold, scurried around, drew a huge spider on black construction paper and glued it to the wall. At which point, filled with satis-faction that I could now act with integrity by telling the truth, I pointed proudly to the spider I helped to create, and with a grand, dramatic flourish intoned loudly: "Look, there's a spider on the wall. That's all!"

I can still recall the feeling of power and accomplish-ment, as parents chuckled with delight and the au-dience applauded. I think I decided then and there that school was a great place, and I liked the feeling of having a positive impact on a group of people.

By the age of three-and-a-half, I became annoyed that the adults around me could read and I couldn't. They read newspapers and street signs and bedtime stories to me. I listened, but could only decipher the pictures and not the words in the books. So I decided to embrace books. In fact, I carried the first grade primer my mother gave me everywhere I went. And I implored her always to teach me to read. She gladly accommodated me.

At that point I once again became impatient. I wasn't yet enrolled in school, even though I could read (and write). My cousins went to school; why couldn't I? So my mother used her influence to get the headmistress at her school to make an exception and enroll me in kindergarten class at age three, instead of four. I organized a group of children in my class, and spent all my free time conducting my own school-within-a-school teaching these children everything I knew.

These early childhood accomplishments were rewarded and nurtured by proud parents who regularly paraded me in front of guests to recite poetry or participate in "adult" discussions about politics and my own budding brand of philosophy. High achievement both academically and in sports seemed to come effortlessly over the next decade of my life and I enjoyed great popularity as a member of the debate team and a host of other extracurricular activities.

Then, at age fifteen, the bottom fell out of my world.

My family migrated to New York City, and I had to
start all over in a strange, new culture; lifelong
friends left behind; feeling too self-conscious about
my foreign accent to join the debate team or speak
in front of a group; having my self-esteem seriously
challenged for the first time since my stage debut at
age three. I struggled for two years to regain my
equilibrium. I immersed myself in the one area that
I knew held positive rewards: academic excellence. I
buried myself in books and school-related activities,
including the risky business of joining the debate
team in spite of my trepidation about my "differ-
ence." I was elected class president in my senior year
of high school in this strange new culture, and
graduated with flying colors, the idea of teaching for
a living etched indelibly in my consciousness.

The above are highlights of two stories from the first
seventeen years of my life. I am very aware of how who I
am and how I lead was influenced by these seminal experiences. If I were to chart my first ten years of life, it would
look like the summary that follows:

AGE 0–10

Critical Life Event	My Feelings
Stage debut at age three	Anxiety followed by the thrill of achievement. Positive feedback (applause) felt wonderfully affirming.

Key Persons (Guides, Allies, Detractors)*	My Personal Choices
Mother, teachers, and students	I decided to perform.

Results	My Lessons Learned
I got positive affirmation in the form of a standing ovation.	I can make choices and thereby influence outcomes in my life.
I got data that said "being on stage" and teaching are positive experiences.	To be effective, it helps to pay attention to your impact on others.

*Notes on this process of self-reflection:

1. While I'm suggesting you do this exercise as a way of taking stock of the lessons of your entire life so far, notice that these charts can be replicated and used in any situation—an important staff meeting, an invitation to resign your current position, the loss of a loved one, and so forth.

2. A word about KEY PERSONS: sometimes these are actual people; sometimes these are inner guides or inner demons such as loneliness or fear. The roles these play are important because they are our teachers whether they happen to be for or against us.

3. Zen philosophers teach us that "pain is a given, but suffering is a choice." Notice that the notations in the first column of this chart are basically "objective." Events and people show up in our lives with or without our mindful choice, and results occur—stuff, sometimes painful, "happens" in our lives. The notations in the column on the right are about how we respond to the stuff and what we might learn in the process.

4. Notice the focus on the individual in the right-hand column. You get the most out of this process if you attend to *your* feelings, *your* choices (not the choices made for you by someone else, but *your* choice in response to that event, if it happens), and finally, the lessons *your* life is teaching you.

Today, the "spider on the wall" remains part of my personal myth and metaphor. It is one of the rites of passages that has defined and continues to influence my life, my career, and my perspective on things. When delivering keynote addresses, I often reconnect with this childhood experience, especially when others respond positively to my message. Whenever I act with conviction or take a risk, I often recall the little girl on stage and become centered in her power.

Now I invite you to chart your own life lessons and discover your lessons for yourself. For each decade of your life one defining moment—an unforgettable life event that may have changed your perspective and/or your choices forever.

Briefly describe the event or the moment in the square titles "Critical Life Event." Continue filling in the appropriate boxes. Note your feelings, key persons involved, personal choices (if applicable), the results or impact on your life, and the lessons learned.

Next comes the fun part: for the years beyond your current age, project into the future, filling in the boxes with what you hope your future years will bring.

You can be as detailed as you would like to be. Invite someone close to you to participate in the exercise, if you wish. Then you can take turns talking about your life lessons: the highs, the lows, and the lessons learned or strengths discovered in each case. I have provided blank charts on the following pages for your convenience in doing this important self-knowledge exercise. Feel free to reproduce these charts and use them as a tool for self-reflection in other situations as well.

AGE 0–10

Critical Life Event	My Feelings
Key Persons (Guides, Allies, Detractors)	My Personal Choices
Results	My Lessons Learned

AGE 11–15

Critical Life Event	My Feelings

Key Persons (Guides, Allies, Detractors)	My Personal Choices

Results	My Lessons Learned

AGE 16—20

Critical Life Event	My Feelings

Key Persons (Guides, Allies, Detractors)	My Personal Choices

Results	My Lessons Learned

AGE 21–30

Critical Life Event	My Feelings
Key Persons (Guides, Allies, Detractors)	My Personal Choices
Results	My Lessons Learned

AGE 31–40

Critical Life Event	My Feelings
Key Persons (Guides, Allies, Detractors)	My Personal Choices
Results	My Lessons Learned

AGE 41–50

Critical Life Event	My Feelings
Key Persons (Guides, Allies, Detractors)	My Personal Choices
Results	My Lessons Learned

AGE 51—60

Critical Life Event	My Feelings
Key Persons (Guides, Allies, Detractors)	My Personal Choices
Results	My Lessons Learned

AGE 61–75

Critical Life Event	My Feelings
Key Persons (Guides, Allies, Detractors)	My Personal Choices
Results	My Lessons Learned

AGE 76–85

Critical Life Event	My Feelings
Key Persons (Guides, Allies, Detractors)	My Personal Choices
Results	My Lessons Learned

AGE 86–100

Critical Life Event	My Feelings
Key Persons (Guides, Allies, Detractors)	My Personal Choices
Results	My Lessons Learned

Now, return to the charts and peruse them with a different lens. I invite you to go deeper and get more creative. Remove your "analytic" mind and call in your "intuitive" mind for the following questions:

1. What are the recurring themes in your life? What metaphor would you use to describe your life?
2. What surprises you the most about this exercise?
3. What concerns you? What thought patterns and behaviors tend to trip you up?
4. What pleases you? What thought patterns and behaviors tend to free and motivate you?
5. What personal strengths seem apparent? What do you notice about how you "lead" in difficult situations?
6. What would you like to celebrate about your life?
7. What lesson (or lessons) is your life trying to teach you right now?
8. Based on this, what have you been lying to yourself about?
9. If you were to target one area for personal development or special attention, based on this exercise what would it be?
10. What is the risk you need to take to be a more effective leader in your own life?

Leadership, Followership, and Motivation

Life coevolves. . . . Even as we draw the boundary of self, we also are creating an environment for others to participate in. We separate ourselves, but we also create the conditions for another's life. One self-asserting being creates itself, and its presence creates conditions for others to take form.

—MARGARET J. WHEATLEY *and*
MYRON KENNER-ROGERS, *A Simpler Way*

This book focuses on the *inner* work of leadership development. But leadership can only be truly understood in the context of the *outer* work of human relationships. In the end, leadership involves getting change to happen *with* and *through* others. Whether discussing vertical (top down) leadership, or horizontal (peer, team, shared) leadership, I use the term "leader" to describe anyone who in a given instance inspires and promotes positive change by engaging followers or enabling them to exercise leadership in their own right.

My bias says that the best leaders are motivated not just by their own purpose, but take into account the needs and motives of others as well. By this definition, leadership, followership, and motivation are inextricably linked. The three are connected not only because leaders must be guided by followers' concerns, but because it is the followers' perception of the leader's character and skills that determines the level of trust, and therefore the willingness to engage—to be motivated. Followers, in a sense, empower leaders to lead simply by deciding to follow.

Where there is no followership—no demonstrated change or goal attainment—there is no leadership. Where there is no leadership—no passion, purpose, trustworthiness, and competence—there is no followership. Leadership and followership are opposite sides of the same coin. You can "lead" all you want, but if you are unable to garner committed "followership" around a vision and to direct your own and others' performance toward achievement of the related goals and plans, you are not exercising leadership.

This understanding of the leader/follower connection is critical today. We now live in a climate where the meaning of family, workplace, marketplace, and community is challenged and changing rapidly. As these shifts have occurred, followers and leaders have experienced broken promises and a loss of trust. To regain our footing and secure the future we want, we must forge new leader/follower relationships.

Furthermore, you can only lead for as long as followers will permit—for as long as they see you as a credible and trustworthy source of influence. A "follower," as the term is used throughout this book, needn't be subordinate in an organizational sense to the leader. A follower is anyone who feels empowered by the leader's vision and example, and who is therefore committed to working jointly toward shared goals. At times, the followers may be your boss, the board of directors, your children, constituents whom you affect positively through your lobbying efforts, or your employees.

Management, leadership, and followership are, of course, all situational. At times, the effective leader must put all of his or her energies into managing. That's what it takes to **implement and secure the vision**. At times, the leader must step out in front of the pack, taking risks and championing new causes. At other times, *the leader must follow.* In fact, **the best leaders are good followers**. They seek input; they ask for help; they are able to modify their position when they discover that their choices are ill advised. They are able to give away power, and in so doing invite their followers to participate in shared leadership—a pooling of everyone's talents towards the common goal.

From the Leadership Perspective . . .

We are all aware that formal organization leaders—the ones with decision-making clout and executive status—have a unique charge that differs from that of the rest of the workforce. They are held responsible and accountable for the marshalling and deployment of resources in service of the enterprise's goals. They must set direction. They must create a motivating environment that will inspire and support people to *want* to move in the envisioned direction. They must be willing to challenge the status quo when change is called for and see to it that people have the skills, resources, and rewards that will direct attention and commitment towards a shared vision.

John Gardner, founding chairman of the think tank Common Cause and an exemplary leader in his own right, devoted his time for many years to the study of leadership. In the first of several pamphlets on leadership, he defines it as *"the process of persuasion and example by which an individual (or leadership team) induces a group to take action that is in accord with the leader's purposes or the shared purposes of all."*

Peter Drucker, world-renowned management scholar, takes yet another approach to explaining leadership and how leaders emerge. Drucker has taught us that leadership has little to do with special qualities such as charisma; it is simply performance. "More doing than dash." By this definition, the person who perceives an opportunity or fills a need emerges as a leader, provided he or she meets the expectations of followers.

Influenced by James MacGregor Burns's work on leadership in the late 1970s, Warren Bennis and Burt Nanus explore the concept of "transformative leadership" in their book, *Leaders*. They describe this contemporary version of the leader as *"one who commits people to action, who converts followers into leaders, and who may convert leaders into agents of change."* In the final chapter of their book, Bennis and Nanus talk about the "symbiotic relationship between leaders and followers," and suggest that for transformative leadership to occur the leader must *"reflect the community of interests of both leaders and followers."*

They then go on to make the now often quoted distinction between managing and leading: "Managers are people who do things right, and leaders are people who do the right thing. The difference may be summarized as activities of vision and judgment—effectiveness—versus activities of mastering routines—efficiency."

More recently, James Kouzes and Barry Posner have offered us perhaps the most compelling compendium of exemplary leadership behaviors, based on huge data bases collected by observing leaders in every sector. They make an important distinction between "managing" and "leading": getting people to *do* versus getting them to *want* to do. But here is what their research teaches us about leadership practices: leaders at their best are seen to consistently exhibit behaviors that can be summarized under five categories. These categories are: challenging the process, inspiring a shared vision, enabling others to act, modeling the way, and encouraging the heart. This material, discussed in the best-selling authors' books *The Leadership Challenge* and their more recent *Encouraging The Heart: A Leader's Guide to Rewarding and Recognizing Others*, has added a much needed dimension to our understanding of leadership from both leaders' and followers' perspectives.

From the Followership Perspective . . .

As discussed above, formal, vertical leaders are expected to be stewards of the enterprise on behalf of customers, constituents, shareholders, and community. In today's leadership climate, they are expected to exhibit certain characteristics and competencies: integrity, enthusiasm, resilience under pressure, leading-edge thinking, awareness of the external environment, people skills, technical credibility, creativity, and courage, to name a few. *But so is everyone else in a sense.* If you are a "follower," your decision to cooperate and to align yourself with the enterprise's goals and strategy (or not to do so) comprises an act of personal leadership. If in the course of your work or in a staff meeting you identify a difficulty and persuasively offer up an alternative course of action that is accepted, you are participating in shared leadership as well. In developing themselves, exemplary employees focus on the same personal characteristics and competencies as formal leaders, in varying degrees, of course.

Robert Kelley, a noted Carnegie-Mellon business school professor and leadership scholar, and I appeared as copanelists once at a forum sponsored by the Pittsburgh-based Executive Report. He was to speak to the nature of "followership" and I was to speak to the nature of "leadership." We ended up saying pretty much the same kinds of things. Kelley discussed four qualities of effective followers. Interestingly, these qualities epitomize leadership as well:

1. They manage themselves well.
2. They commit to the organization and to a purpose, principle, or person outside themselves.
3. They build their competence and focus their efforts for maximum impact.
4. They are courageous, honest, and credible.

In Kelley's view leadership and followership are "equal but different activities."

Writing about the power of the follower in today's "new workforce," Robert Kelley says in his book, *The Gold Collar Worker*, that new work ethics—"risk-taking, tolerance, mutual respect, responsible participation, interdependence, balance between professional and extracurricular pursuits, and a high quality of life"—guide the expectations of many professionals. He goes on to add: "They want a good job but are less driven by the external rewards of promotion and status. They are not innocently attracted to power, nor do they want to follow." This interesting perspective would challenge our assumptions about traditional leadership.

A leader, says John Gardner in subsequent papers, cannot be viewed separately from followers. Followers, by their consent to follow, call forth the leader. **One rises to leadership and continues to lead only so long as followers empower one to do so.** This claim holds the key to "motivation," for it suggests that a leader induces commitment from followers if the leader clearly demonstrates his or her willingness to help followers meet their needs.

Motivation

Leadership is ultimately measured by the leader's impact on lives—his or her own as well as others'. As suggested throughout this book, transformation of our outer world, or our ability to serve others through leadership, begins with self-transformation. Again the practice of self-reflection is the key ingredient. By reflecting on our life patterns and life lessons, we come to know ourselves more intimately. We become clear about our values, our motives, our unique talents, and the ways in which we are called to serve in our families, our communities, the work world, or the planet. As we journey inward to know ourselves as leaders, we must consider questions of drives and motives: What propels me to take initiative? What drives me as I attempt to influence outcomes in my life and the lives of others?

If you look back over your Life Mapping exercise in the previous chapter, you may notice that the defining question in each decade or two of your life changes. In your childhood, your life may have been defined by questions like, How can I survive? As you enter adulthood, you are more likely to be motivated by questions of success: How can I thrive? Later in your life, as you face predictable crises that call for major self-renewal, questions of transcendence will present themselves: How can I find deeper meaning? How can I connect more deeply with my purpose, my passion, and my wisdom? Of course, as I suggested in Chapter 3, some people get stuck at basic survival levels and do not necessarily pursue the latter questions. But if we are to emerge as truly effective leaders, we must be open to pursuing an understanding of ourselves and our passion and drives.

In Chapter 2, I posed the question: Why do some people choose to lead while others follow—or still others do neither? In other words, **what motivates people to take action?** We have all heard incredible stories of people who perform superhuman feats in a crisis. A *Time Magazine* article several years ago reported the story of a frail, ailing mother who lifted a 3,300-pound station wagon to release her son who was pinned beneath it. In situations like this, mind and body combine to evoke a stress fight-or-flight response. The release of adrenalin, cortisone, endorphins, and other body chemicals needed to prepare the muscles, the circulatory systems, and the brain to act in ways not normally possible is the physical part of the equation. But there is a mental and spiritual component, too. In moments like these, we observe the human organism at peak performance—able to garner all the gumption, passion, and power needed to take transformative action.

Highly motivated people replicate such behaviors, perhaps in more modest ways, every day. They do so with support from others and with the personal power that comes from their inner journey to tap the leader in themselves. Barbara Grogan, founder of Western Industrial Contractors, a $6 million a year millwrighting firm in Denver, is an interesting example of how motivation can spark impressive action. At age thirty-five, faced with the crisis of divorce, she transformed her life from that of an insecure woman to a wealthy entrepreneur. Armed with a psychology degree, very little money, and even less experience, she chose to start a contracting business because she thought no one would hire her. Since contracting allowed her to lease equipment and subcontract business on a project-by-project basis, it required very little start-up capital. So she plunged in, paradoxically motivated by fear and the need to feed her children.

When we observe the behavior of people in crisis who choose to take control of the situation, the definition of motivation becomes clearer. The first component of the motivated person's behavior has to do with **focus**. Given the alternatives of action versus inertia, he or she focuses on action. The second component is **persistent effort**. A motivated person directs his or her behavior towards some desired outcome in a **focused** and **persistent way**.

"Motivating" Others

Marketing experts and website designers have taught us a lot about motivation in recent years. When we speak of the "stickiness" of a site, we are concerned with focus and persistence. How do we grab the attention of someone surfing the Web? And how do we "motivate" them to want to stay at the site long enough to be persuaded to buy? In this age of perpetual change, enterprise leaders also face a problem with "stickiness": *how to get employees to stay focused and to commit their effort persistently towards some envisioned outcome.*

While formal leaders tend to be highly motivated, fewer than 25 percent of today's workers claim that they work to their full potential, according to a study by Daniel Yankelovich. I believe that this is due in part to poor leadership. It is also related to the fact that you can't really "motivate" someone else. You can influence their thinking and their experiences in the family, community, or work environment you create. In the words of Kouzes and Posner,

"You can't command commitment, you can only inspire it." Today's formal leaders consistently struggle with how to transform "demotivating" environments into ones that inspire high performance and commitment.

The need for a motivating environment that calls forth the best people have to offer is more pressing than ever. Yet the choices enterprise leaders feel forced to make—downsizing, pay cuts, work overload—are antithetical to the very conditions that lead to high performance. It is difficult for people to remain focused when all around them is changing, when they feel excluded or undervalued. This change-weariness and uncertainty also compromise our ability to put forth our best efforts. We need leaders who can reestablish these two motivating conditions and other related ones needed to reenergize our organizations and their members.

Many of the trainees who participate in my leadership seminars are chosen by their organizations because of their demonstrated managerial and professional skills and their dedication to leadership goals. The course is part of their career development strategy. It is not unusual for these trainees to comment that they are having so much fun or enjoying the challenge of the work so much that their salary is a "bonus" to the real payoffs of the job. Liver transplant pioneer Dr. Thomas Starzl, in discussing his own unswerving motivational level during an NBC news interview, put it this way: "Some people get burnout. Other people only get a stronger desire to make things better. I hope I fit into that category."

Now retired, Starzl is credited with performing more organ transplants than any other surgeon. He accomplished this by taking heroic risks, often putting his entire medical career at stake as he took risks with new procedures or new drugs in his all-consuming attempt to "make things better." Starzl's love of medicine was initially inspired by his mother, a nurse in the small Iowa town where he grew up. His extraordinary vision and persistence are linked to personal character traits that drive him to seek out challenging situations for the sheer thrill of doing something others thought impossible. In fact, he admits he chose his work in medicine specifically with the liver because it is the largest glandular organ—and the most complex.

This intense personal motivation allowed Thomas Starzl to persist amid repeated setbacks, pessimism, and condemnation from medical colleagues at different points in his exemplary career. One of his greatest successes involved FK-506, an immunosuppressant administered to transplant patients to reduce the risk of organ rejection. Again, he pioneered this controversial new treatment amid demands that would diminish the motivation of the bravest souls, and yet he persisted in spite of his own health problems. With his surgical procedures for organ transplantation firmly established in the medical community, Starzl later turned his attention to different research challenges at his transplant institute before retiring.

Motivation is not something that a leader **does** to followers. There are two bodies of research on motivation. Both support the same kind of conclusions about what motivates people—what drives their focused and persistent effort towards a goal. The "content theorists" tell us that specific factors such as our need for safety, inclusion, self-esteem, or personal fulfillment motivate us. "Process theorists" teach that motivation comes from two human dynamics: we receive positive or negative reinforcement (internally or from others) for our actions, or we *believe* we will be rewarded or punished for those actions. The path and behaviors we choose in a given situation are tied to our perception of the likely outcome.

While it is possible for leaders to use reinforcement (reward and punishment) to influence people's behaviors towards some goal, this is not "motivation" in the sense being discussed here. Rewards such as money or perks are a good thing—important to rank-and-file workers and to highly paid executives. When lacking, money and perks become *de-motivators* that cause workers to strike, executives to quit, and employees in general to feel demoralized.

But here is the catch. While worker and CEO alike may desire more money, it is not what necessarily *motivates* them to work harder, better, more creatively. This is especially true when the monetary rewards are not tied *specifically* to performance. The rank-and-file worker needs the cash—needs it badly to make ends meet. For this worker the underlying needs are safety, fairness, personal power, and the like. On the other hand, the seemingly overpaid, seven-figure CEO does not "need" the cash. But similar to the worker, money for the CEO is also tied to more deepseated needs like self-esteem and power. Compensation of that magnitude is a symbolic measure of the CEO's worth in the marketplace and a vote of confidence from the Board. In both cases, the drive is linked more specifically to human factors like survival, safety, fairness, power, and self-esteem.

Organization leaders who understand this are more successful at creating motivating environments. They create work climates that support individual initiative, inclusivity, ownership, creativity, fun—and that compensate people fairly. In such a climate, motivation works best because it is generated intrinsically. It comes from the internal shifts in people that occur when their true needs are being met.

Once these needs are met, it is easier to align self-interests with organizational goals.

When Ralph Dickerson took on the leadership of the United Way of New York City, he was appalled to learn that 45 percent of African American and 60 percent of Hispanic American students drop out between middle school and high school. Recognizing that schools are being given the unreasonable task of "being everything to everyone," and that students arrive with multiple problems beyond the scope of teachers, Dickerson and his leadership team decided to offer a challenge to the Board of Education to do some things differently. The challenge: To get community-based organizations to work with the schools. He set out to create entrepreneurial opportunities for community groups to serve the schools in their own neighborhoods. This would facilitate the process of education on an ongoing basis, both in and out of school.

The joint Board of Education/United Way Advisory Team formed as a result of this vision, motivated the Board of Education to grant $40 million over three years for a project that currently involves eighty schools in the city's toughest neighborhoods, and fifty-four community-based organizations, spawning 119 different programs and affecting 10,000 to 12,000 children and their families. Says Dickerson: "We were able to achieve this by simply laying out a course of action, **taking time to listen** to the Board of Education, the children themselves, the children's families, and the community agencies. We brought these groups together, but it is working because it is driven by their needs and their input."

Richard Nicolosi is often cited as an industry leader whose focus on creating the right business environment motivated employees to transform a declining market into impressive profits against major competition in the eighties. Nicolosi was promoted to Procter & Gamble's Paper Products division at a time when the division's market share for disposable diapers was declining rapidly. Undaunted by slipping profits, he immediately set about empowering all employees to become leaders in their own right. They were supported in developing a team approach in which they were given responsibility well beyond what was typical for the formerly hierarchical bureaucracy Nicolosi inherited. As Nicolosi and his leadership team flattened layer after layer in his organization's hierarchy, they encouraged workers to "shun the incremental and go for the leap." Inspired by Nicolosi's vision and leadership, the work culture changed appreciably as employees became more engaged and more self-directed. The net result: impressive gains in market share for products such as Pampers®, and Luvs® Deluxe and a heightened sense of ownership on the part of employees at all levels.

On the personal level, leaders at their best are **focused** and **persistent**. Their energies are directed. They find personal satisfaction and even joy in what they are pursuing. They become single minded about the cause or the goal they are supporting. They then unleash all their thoughts, emotions, and talents in the desired direction. As they persistently move forward in this state of mind, distractions, disappointments, or setbacks are seen as problems to be solved or as lessons to be learned in order to improve performance. They then continue toward their goal with renewed resolve and heightened awareness.

On the group leadership level, leaders at their best create a motivating environment. They do so by empowering group members to find ways to *align their self-interests with organizational goals*. As demonstrated throughout this book, each individual has a unique set of experiences, and therefore, different personal needs and values. Leaders who understand this respond to group members as individuals, each with his or her own special perspective, each capable of being **focused** and **persistent** in his or her own important way.

Self-Reflection

1. Some people are motivated by the fear of dying. Others are motivated by the joy of living. In which direction do you lean?

2. How does your orientation to life shape your choices as a follower? As a leader?

3. Often I nudge my clients by asking questions like, If you say your children are your first priority, how come you spend so much time at work? If others observed your behavioral choices, what would they think truly motivates you?

4. How consistent is that with how you see yourself?

5. What steps might you take to bring your day-to-day choices into alignment with your true values and motives?

5 Trust: The Cornerstone of Leadership

Trust is a willingness to engage with another in situations that might involve risk or vulnerability. Since leadership, by definition, is aimed at change, trust is the cornerstone of leadership. Every change—every leadership initiative—shakes us loose from our comfort zones. To be positively influenced by someone's leadership we must first trust that person to lead us past our vulnerability and maintain or restore our confidence. We must believe that the leader's intentions towards us are positive and that he or she possesses the ability to get the right results for us. Sure, there are cases where ill-intentioned leaders coerce followers or get compliance based on fear. But, except for those instances, leaders engage followers by demonstrating *trustworthiness*.

These days employees are often change-weary and therefore cynical. It is not surprising that executives are asking, "How do we inspire trust?" For example, in the field of human resources management, emerging research shows that employee engagement (or motivation) is linked to their willingness to trust the leadership. Armed with this awareness, we have broadened our focus on employee satisfaction to include emphasis on "employee engagement." HR surveys now routinely include trust-related items on their rating scales such as, "I am confident that senior management is taking this organization in the right direction."

But how, exactly, does someone come to trust you? Well, the answer is the same whether you are in a formal leadership role such as project manager, or simply setting out to exercise personal leadership to get desired results with colleagues, customers, students, or your relatives. My research has consistently revealed four dimensions of character and behavior that determine whether others see us as trustworthy:

∞ **Competence** (Do you know what you're doing?)

∞ **Integrity** (Do you walk your talk?)

∞ **Goodwill** (Do you show concern for others?)

∞ **Transparency** (Are you a straight-talker?)

Recall a time when you trusted someone unequivocally. Chances are you believed they could be relied on to do the right thing, that they would keep their word, that they had your best interests at heart, and that they were being open and honest with you. Let's further define these four aspects of trust and examine specific attitudes and behaviors associated with each one.

COMPETENCE: *Do You Know What You're Doing?*

Know-how, proficiency, expertise, reliability, experience—these are all words that come to mind when we speak of competence. These words imply that we can count on someone—trust them time after time—to get good results. On work teams we defer to those who demonstrate exemplary problem-solving and decision-making skills. We have confidence in those who can implement effective changes, who bring the right technical expertise on projects, or who have the emotional intelligence and leadership skills needed to consistently achieve performance goals and objectives with and through others.

What's tricky in today's fast changing world, is that we are constantly moving into unexplored territory. Our knowledge base and our technologies become rapidly obsolete and what's required of us in leadership roles is constantly changing. To earn trust by being competent a leader must be ever vigilant. Here are some helpful leadership behaviors to practice:

1. Listen, Learn and Act on What's Learned

Research on grade school children shows that good listeners tend to be high achievers who excel at problem-solving. The same is true of adults in the workplace. Thankfully, it's never too late to become a good listener. It is imperative as competent leaders that we learn to listen and engage in the practice of asking open questions. An open question invites others to freely share their opinions and ideas with you. Imagine a new manager who asks questions such as these: *"What do I need to know about this department in order to be an ally in getting your needs met?"* Or consider the team member who regularly asks: *"How am I doing? What works well? What behaviors do I need to change for us to be more effective as a team?"* The trustworthy leader shores up his or her competence by soliciting feedback and acting on it. Goodwill, another dimension of trust which will be discussed later, also gets generated this way.

A friend of mine who worked in urban planning in New Guinea described to me one of the local leadership practices he observed. While conducting planning meetings, the tribal leader remains silent while everyone else deliberates. He intently listens to the discussion of others and at the end of the deliberations he does one of two things—asks the right question or says "okay, here is what we're going to do." Because he has synthesized all the information from all the different perspectives in the meeting room, he is able to offer a solution or nail just the right question that will lead the parties involved to the best solution. The leader in this culture lives the aphorism: "Seek first to understand, then respond." His deep listening leads to wise decisions, so he gains the trust of those who follow him. He also builds goodwill as he demonstrates that he is open to others and respects their opinions and viewpoints.

Many of us in the position of leadership make the mistake of jumping the gun, asking the wrong question and solving the wrong problem. When we do this, it erodes trust and makes us appear to be incompetent. By asking questions and listening, we demonstrate that we respect the opinions of others and are willing to learn from them. The net results: learning happens and trust is built.

2. Deploy Technical, Financial, and Human Resources Wisely

Whether we're a not-for-profit or government agency, in academia, business, or healthcare we are all dealing with limited resources. Today's world demands that we get better results faster with fewer resources. Outsourcing, offshoring, and now homesourcing are all examples of our current struggle for wise deployment of resources. On the downside of these choices often we find a loss of trust: *"Do these guys know what they're doing?"* beleaguered employees anxious about their future ask, as their jobs are shifted elsewhere. These tough choices pose a possible breach of confidence or a loss of perceived competence that is sure to erode trust.

So the leadership challenge remains how to be innovative and resourceful, able to get the most output from the least input. For example, if you're an executive in a not-for-profit agency with little money, a small staff and lots of people in the community you need to serve, you must think outside the boundaries of funding limitations and ask, where else can I get resources to help us deliver on our promise to the community? If you are operating with competence you may consider going to a community college to recruit students to work as volunteers and interns. This is a win-win situation, the students get job-related experience and your non-profit gets fresh talent at no additional cost.

3. Get the Job Done Well and on Time

Peter Drucker rightly said, "leadership is more doing than dash." One of the ways that we demonstrate competence as leaders is to actually do what we say we will do. If you have a project that you believe you can complete by mid-July, give yourself two additional weeks to get the job done. This allows you time to manage the unforeseen, do your best work, and minimize your stress level. And if you do, in fact complete the job earlier than promised, you wow your customer and earn their trust.

Sometimes we fall victim to procrastination and lose our credibility as a result. When you find yourself dragging your feet on "important" things, you need to be self-reflective and ask yourself, is this something I *really* want to do? Sometimes, when we procrastinate, it is because we are attempting activities that our souls really don't want to be engaged in. You may be late to work everyday; but early when it's time to meet your friends at the golf course. Ask yourself what being late for work really says about your priorities? Could it be your job is not a right fit and your soul is telling you that you need to change jobs? Earlier in life, I believed I wanted to be a poet; but always put off completing my collection of poems and getting it published. I eventually had to face up to the fact that my procrastination was a sign that I really didn't want to be a poet—at least not that way. I now find ways to incorporate the part of me that is poetic into my book writing and speaking, and I *readily* share my ideas with the world this way.

4. Make Learning a Lifelong Priority

It's always surprising to me when I come into an organization and discover many senior level staff embarrassed to be seen in an educational workshop. Effective leaders actively seek out learning opportunities. They are willing to admit the limits of their knowledge and to ask for input. They are constantly reading or listening to books on tape. But they also recognize that learning does not just come from books or formal studies, although both are important. They relish information from multiple sources and are not embarrassed to ask, "How do you do that?" or "What do I need to learn to be more effective in my work?" Exemplary leaders demonstrate to people that they're worthy of being followed because they are either in the know, or are willing to learn. Most importantly, they regularly look inward to reflect on lessons learned from life lessons.

Years ago I watched a popular talk show that featured a woman who had been married six times. Each husband was a physically abusive alcoholic. It was apparent to everyone in the audience that she was making the same mistake over and over again. But because she was not self-reflective enough to see her mistakes and learn from them, she could not break the pattern. If she had been self-reflective, she would have asked herself, "What is it that I am doing that is attracting this pattern in my life?" Our capacity to self-reflect is not only linked to personal power as discussed elsewhere in this book, it is also linked to our ability to earn trust by applying the wisdom gained from life lessons.

The life mapping exercise you completed earlier in this book dramatizes the power of life as a teacher. By reflecting on your "lessons learned" responses you can make more conscious choices about how to apply these insights to demonstrate leadership competence.

5. Build Sound Interpersonal Relationships

Ultimately trustworthiness and leadership are measured by our *impact* on others. If you're like me you've probably run across a supervisor in your life who has said, "You don't have to like me, just respect me!" That statement is the most arrogant and foolish thing a supervisor could ever say. For anyone to expect respect without building sound interpersonal relationships shows a glaring lack of interpersonal competence. To be trustworthy we must build sound interpersonal relationships that allow people to say, "I may not like the decision you made; but I trust your good intentions and your humanity." This way we can get the job done and preserve our good working relationships even when decisions have been made that ruffle feathers.

Sound relationships also require a willingness to self-disclose. If you know you're under pressure and there is a lack of resources, let your direct reports and colleagues know. If you don't yet have full information say, "This is the best information I have right now. When I learn more, I will get back to you with an update." Then, of course, be sure to follow through.

INTEGRITY: *Do You Walk Your Talk?*

In addition to competence, trust hinges on integrity—a willingness to speak the truth, a penchant for keeping promises, and the practice of acting in ways that are aligned with our stated values and beliefs. To demonstrate integrity we must hold true to our commitments, whether those commitments are to self or to others. We must be clear about our principles or values and have the courage to live those values consistently. In fact, the word "integrity" literally means "wholeness" and implies that a person has aligned their inner and outer lives, including the various aspects of their personality, preferences, and behaviors into a harmonious whole. Given this definition, it is not surprising that integrity is at the core of trust. In fact, at times the term is synonymous with trust itself. Below is a list of observable behaviors associated with integrity:

1. Be Honest and Ethical in Dealing with Others

One of the biggest challenges for leaders today is that we live in a rapidly changing business, government and global environment. Because of this, just as quickly as we've given our word, this rapidly changing landscape proves us a liar. Managers may say to workers, "We're going to have to offshore 30% of our jobs," only to be forced to come back a month later and say, "Oops, it's now 50%." Although the manager may have intended to give correct information based on the facts at the time, such changes, if not handled with integrity, will certainly erode trust. To prevent this requires honesty and the sensitivity that comes from a willingness to walk in others' shoes. A more accurate message might be, "These are tough times where things change without notice. Our plan is to offshore 30% of the business, but that could change. So we will keep you posted." Then, of course, to maintain integrity, the manager in this scenario must keep his or her word, getting back to people quickly, openly and honestly.

2. Make Promises You Can Keep

To maintain integrity be realistic with your promises and willing to let people know when things change. If you are caught in a cycle of promising too much and therefore not able to deliver all you'd hoped to, take steps to reverse the pattern. Be more realistic. Promise less. Weigh your situation and your resources carefully, then give yourself ample time to fulfill your promise. Then if you are able to deliver sooner than promised, you delight your customer and yourself. On the (hopefully rare) occasions when you find yourself unable to keep a promise, let the other person know immediately and renegotiate new expectations. Don't wait until the last possible minute to tell your project manager that the project is over budget. If you are thinking of saying, "Yes" to a request to serve on yet another committee and everything inside of you screams, "No!" listen to your gut. Be honest with yourself and others. Reconsider whether this is a promise you can keep with integrity and be willing to say no. (To preserve the relationship, you may want to suggest alternatives or help identify someone else to do the job.) By stopping to check your internal compass, your actions in the outer world will be congruent with your true feelings, values, and needs. This alignment is at the heart of integrity.

3. Admit Mistakes and Weak Points

When you admit your weaknesses and mistakes it shows others that you are human and honest. It builds trust and engages followers much more easily. If you make a mistake, admit it and ask—"what can I do to improve this?" This is not an open invitation to go around self-flagellating yourself in public and pointing out any and everything you could possibly do wrong, because that will surely erode trust. But be honest with yourself and others about your strong points and weak points. I'm a big picture person. When it comes to the overall vision I'm great, but when faced with the nuts and bolts of implementation, I quickly lose interest. I know that my strong suit is not in the details. So when working on projects with others, I surround myself with those who have a knack for details. When in the position of leadership we need to recognize our strengths and weaknesses so that others can feel invited to complement you with their skills.

4. Check to Make Sure That Your Impact on Others Matches Your Intentions

There is a commonly used phrase in business, "We judge ourselves by our intentions; but others judge us by our impact." Often, when we have an unintended negative impact on others we will say, "Well you know that's not what I meant." But to say that is never enough. Instead of saying, "Well you know that's not what I meant" when someone tells you that your impact is less than desirable, ask, "What was the behavior I engaged in that had that kind of impact?" Then make a mental note to try a different behavior next time.

If you're working as an editor on a writer's manuscript and mark their paper with huge question marks and negative comments in red pen, your intention may be to make this piece of writing the best possible; but your impact most likely will be to demoralize the writer and make him or her feel overwhelmed with a sense that their writing will never be good enough. By checking in with the writer, you are likely to get useful feedback about the impact of your choices. You can then make sure, in the future, that your critique of the writer's work has the desired impact by perhaps making corrections in green pen and finding what is right with the work and adding those positive comments as well.

If you're in management you may be making choices about the firm that will have long-term positive effects on the company; but your short-term impact may leave employees feeling overworked and undervalued. You may create the desired impact on employees by getting feedback from them, asking, "What can I do to support you in making this transition as painless as possible?"

5. Consistently Live Your Stated Values and Vision

As discussed earlier, integrity means your walk (how you act) is congruent with your talk (what you say you believe in). If you say you value excellence, you would not turn in a report riddled with typos. If you say you value others, then you would not trample on people as you make your way to the top of the organization. If you say you value the opinions of others, then you need to be self-reflective and ask yourself and others, "Am I truly a good listener?" If you truly care about how your management decisions have affected others, ask employees, "How have these decisions affected the quality of your work experience?" One of the easiest ways to make sure that you are consistently walking the talk is to ask for honest and open feedback. Once you receive the feedback, if you realize that your actions are not consistent with what you say you value, take immediate steps to put yourself in alignment.

GOODWILL: *Do You Show Concern for Others?*

Put simply, goodwill means caring about others and showing it. This dimension of trust, also labeled "benevolence," quickly comes under scrutiny when leaders make decisions. The first thing that people ask when facing change is, "How is this going to impact me?" They wonder if leaders actually care about the well-being of those asked to execute the changes or of those impacted by it. To generate goodwill, consistently treat people as *they* would like to be treated. Figure out what people need and be sensitive and supportive in helping them get their needs met. If the people you seek to influence believe that you have their best interests at heart they are more likely to trust you.

Interestingly, in the business sense of the word, "goodwill" is an accounting term used to describe the value of an entity beyond its tangible assets. This means that over time, the business has amassed a future potential to do well because past and present customers have consistently supported the business. It is assumed that this customer vote of confidence (or trust) comes in direct response to good business practices—product superiority, excellence in customer service, and the like. The same holds true for our routine interactions with people. The following are a few behaviors that, if practiced with integrity, will foster trust by building goodwill.

1. Show Respect for Colleagues and Clients

In employee engagement surveys, respect is among the most common aspect of working relationships that employees are concerned about. They seek it, but often find it lacking from supervisors, colleagues, and direct reports. Where respect is lacking, trust is lost. Respect means we honor the rights of others, treat them with dignity and care, and value the talents, skills, perspectives and needs of others. Respect is easily evidenced when we believe that others are valuable as human beings and are willing to engage them not in spite of their differences; but *because of* their differences.

Some years ago, I worked with a healthcare facility where many employees complained that senior level staff did not take the time to get to know lower level staff or solicit their input about patient care or the work environment. They gave examples such as senior level employees not remembering the names of entry to mid level colleagues with whom they worked for many years. This created a "classist" environment where staff did not feel respected. The result: eroded trust.

As leaders, how do we know if we are being respectful? Ask yourself, "Do I make an effort to remember staff members' names?" "Do I say good morning?" "Do I seek input and ideas from those who are less credentialed and treat their perspective as valid and useful? In my busy work day do I take the extra moment to make eye-contact, to say 'please,' or 'thank you,' or simply acknowledge someone for a job well done?"

2. Be Fair and Supportive When Dealing with Others

Inequity in how people are treated, especially in the workplace destroys goodwill. As leaders we need to use the same standard of fairness across the board. When giving constructive feedback, deliver it in a way that is descriptive, not judgmental and describe the impact of that person's actions. If the person is chronically late, say, "When you arrive late at a meeting, I have a problem with that because I'm afraid you may miss important information." When someone offers a suggestion, take the time to consider it carefully before discounting it. Perhaps that worker on the front line has a perspective that management could benefit from. If, as a supervisor, you routinely give parents time off for family matters, or spare them the challenges of business trips, consider that workers without children also have a life and need downtime as well.

On occasion, rolling your sleeves up and diving in to work with subordinates during a crunch is one of the most effective ways of building goodwill in the workplace. A leader, who is not above getting into the trenches, quickly becomes endeared to colleagues and direct reports. When you are fair with others, especially in your feedback, the person walks away feeling supported and respected.

3. Listen Attentively Especially When Others' Viewpoints, Backgrounds and Experiences Differ from Your Own

Listening is the greatest gift of goodwill. You will never hear anyone say, "You listen too much." The fastest way to build goodwill is to listen attentively and sincerely to what others have to say, even if you don't agree. Before sharing your viewpoint, repeat back to the other person what they said and allow them to confirm that they actually said what you heard. You say, "Let me see if I understand what you're saying . . ." and only after they have confirmed what you heard is correct do you follow with your opinion. This type of interaction leaves all parties feeling affirmed and is a contributing factor to goodwill. Most importantly, this leadership behavior builds effective working relationships and assures that you will make wiser decisions as you attempt to make a difference in whatever you do.

4. Show Camaraderie and Warmth

In today's world we've lost the ability to be playful, fun loving and spontaneous with each other, especially in the workplace. Life is moving so rapidly that many people are becoming humorless, forgetting how to laugh at themselves, with others, or to even recall a funny story during a meeting. It is easier to zip through our workday or through interactions with others in any setting without pausing to acknowledge some need or some difficulty another may be having. Add to that the tensions that come from living in fear-evoking, litigious environments, and you get a picture that is less and less conducive to goodwill.

I met a young man who attended a sexual harassment training moderated by lawyers that was so fear evoking that he found himself second guessing his actions around female co-workers. He refused to close the door to his office if a female co-worker requested to meet with him. He said that a co-worker's husband died in a motorcycle accident, he started to hug her but caught himself. How sad that he no longer felt free to express appropriate compassion toward a fellow human being because his spontaneity and goodwill was replaced by fear.

It is impossible for camaraderie and warmth to exist in an environment where people find themselves measuring every action; where they are told "take risks, but you better not fail," or where they can't be generous, forgiving or playful with each other. As leaders we need to invite neoteny back into our workplaces. Neoteny means to be child-like, spontaneous and fun loving; but appropriate—not child*ish*. We need to model the way so it's clear what is acceptable and what isn't, then trust that our workers can make appropriate judgments about how they should interact with one another.

5. Acknowledge People's Accomplishments

So often, we focus on finding out what people are doing wrong. To build goodwill we need to focus on how we can catch people doing things *right*. Practice giving feedback about what works well; what a great friend someone is, what an effective decision your boss or a colleague just made, what a great life partner your spouse is, and so forth. But when you give such feedback make sure that you are telling the truth. If this is done as a sham, others will quickly see you as disingenuous, and it will actually diminish, rather than build goodwill and trust.

Also when you take steps to reward others for their contributions, be sure to match the rewards to what people really need or desire. Many leaders make the mistake of believing that we all want to be rewarded the same way, so they schedule a Saturday golf outing or hand out free mugs without thinking about how those rewards affect others. Many workers, especially single parents, may not be able to find a babysitter for a Saturday golf outing and a lot of people have more than enough free mugs cluttering their cabinets. Get into the habit of asking others what's meaningful to them. When you ask others how they want to be treated they feel part of a team that values and celebrates them and their contributions.

TRANSPARENCY: *Are You a Straight-Talker?*

Transparency refers to the way in which we communicate with others. To become a transparent communicator we must be willing to disclose our true feelings, intentions, needs and observations. Self-disclosure increases camaraderie, puts people at ease, and gives them better quality information. Transparent communicators are readily experienced as trustworthy.

The modern world is so flush with information and rapid changes that most don't have time to communicate well. We communicate on the fly; with a quick smile, a hurried hello in the hallways, or a cryptic email filled with buzz words and acronyms. Trust is earned if people believe that your communication is thoughtful, honest and sincere. Are you guilty of organization double-talk in the midst of a change effort? Do you self-disclose and use straight talk? Is your message consistent? Here are some ideas that will help you achieve congruence between your true feelings, and your communication with others.

1. Share Full Information Whenever Possible

Sharing full information does not mean you are free to violate confidentiality. It means you strive, wherever possible, to make sure people have the best, most complete information possible to do a good job. It means you trust others' capacity to handle the truth and that you understand how information sharing links to team effectiveness, innovation and relationship-building.

If you are working as a manager and privy to the inner workings of your organization, then as you delegate work to your direct reports, make sure that you communicate to them why they are doing something so they understand why their work is important to the business strategy. A positive side effect of this is that workers then feel valued and valuable to the organization. They are more likely to take initiative, surface their best ideas and trust that decision-makers see and respect their competence. Conversely, when we fail to share full information, people create their own version of the truth, circulate it through the employee grapevine, damaging morale and team performance.

2. Communicate Clearly and Candidly

Effective leaders use straight talk and communicate with the world in a way that is candid yet nonjudgmental. Avoid double negatives such as, "I don't disagree with you," or "It's not that I don't trust you." These types of statements mean nothing, they only communicate that you are not willing to express what you really think. Instead of saying "I don't disagree with you," say, "I agree with this part of what you're saying but not with the rest." Or instead of saying "It's not that I don't trust you," you might say "The last three times I gave you an assignment, it was three weeks late, so I don't trust that this assignment will be on time." Avoid using insider information, acronyms and language that others don't understand. If you must use this type of language make sure that you thoroughly explain it so that your listener understands.

3. Be Honest about Your Observations and Expectations

The transparent leader strives to reveal true thoughts, feelings, expectations, and observations. If you're conducting a meeting and notice that certain members are cutting each other off, interject. Name the behavior and try to resolve it. It is only when we fail to be transparent about our feelings, thoughts, and observations that we end up with the parking lot meeting after the meeting which, over time, certainly erodes trust.

Use "I" language, and avoid "you" and "we" language when expressing how you feel. If you intend to share a true feeling, don't use the phrase "I feel *that*" because once you insert the word "that" you are sharing an opinion, not a feeling. Instead say: "I feel frustrated . . ." or "I feel angry and undervalued right now . . ." Then go on to explain why being descriptive, not judgmental, of the person with whom you are communicating.

Finally, make sure that you go beyond expressing your feelings by being clear and helpful in describing your expectations in the future. For example, instead of simply saying, "We just don't communicate well on this team." Be explicit: "We need to listen more intently and explore our differences before rushing to judgment during our team meetings."

4. Talk with People, Not about Them Behind Their Backs

The parking lot meeting after the meeting is one of the most common occurrences in a workplace where trust has been eroded. Often workers will have a problem with a co-worker, or change in the workplace. Instead of going to that co-worker or manager, they go to others who add fuel to the fire by sharing their negative experiences. Because of fear, many people hesitate to give feedback to others about behavior that impacted them negatively, so they vent instead of trying to solve the problem. Sometimes we need to vent, but then it's our responsibility to share our feelings directly with the person who has offended us. Or, if you are on the listening end of the vent, you need to tell the person venting, "Okay, have you told them how you feel?" It takes courage to give feedback to others, especially if that feedback is a critique. A true leader feels the discomfort of having to give feedback to others, and pushes through the fear by talking to them anyway.

5. Give Honest, Timely, Constructive Feedback

When giving feedback to others give it right away, right after you see the behavior. Don't go talk to several other colleagues first. Be constructive. Saying "I just don't like you because you remind me of my mother," is not a constructive statement. "I don't like it when you ignore what I've said, it makes me feel invisible; please acknowledge what I have said before giving your opinion," is a statement someone can take action on. Don't sugarcoat your statements by saying "don't take this the wrong way; but . . ." or "I hope you don't take this personally . . ." Because when you do that you are telling this person that you see them as a fragile human being who is incapable of handling constructive feedback. Before you give them feedback, ask for their permission. You may say, "I want to give you some feedback about something, is that okay?" Or in the beginning of your relationship you might want to tell them, "I want you to be honest and open with me about anything that I do that you may like or dislike, is it okay if I do the same with you?"

6. Ask for Feedback and Reward It

Giving and receiving feedback are perhaps the most difficult communication skills for all of us. We are rarely taught these skills as we learn to speak, read, and write. To compound things our egos—the part of our psyches that deludes us into thinking we are perfect, or ought to be—makes it less likely that we will ask for feedback, whether positive or corrective. We especially fear corrective, or "negative," feedback. We tend to receive such feedback as criticisms that threaten our idealized self-image. We also shy away from giving corrective feedback for fear that we may damage a fragile relationship in the process. Sadly, our trepidation about giving and receiving feedback sets us up to experience the very thing we fear—a loss of trust.

To keep feedback coming, you must reward it. Whether you agree with the feedback or not, avoid being defensive. Instead allow yourself time to reflect on it. Avoid the classic defensive response: *"How can you say that I'm defensive! I'm not defensive."* Instead say, "Thanks for the feedback. I'll think about it, then we can talk about it further." Ironically, sometimes when you find yourself getting defensive it's likely the person giving the feedback has hit a nerve because there is some truth to their statement, so sit with the feedback for a while and observe your subsequent behaviors before shooting the messenger. If, after careful reflection, you find truth in what the person said, go back to them and say, "You were right," and make that person an ally in your leadership growth by asking him or her to help you monitor your behavior.

I once took the bold step of asking my adult son to give me feedback on my parenting. He shared memories of things I said or did that were major for him, but were insignificant to me at the time. He complimented me on parenting behaviors that I thought I was lousy at, and revealed some ineffective choices I had made about which I was totally unaware. That conversation was an eye-opener, revealing much about my parent-as-leader approach. My only regret was not having asked for this feedback years earlier.

Without feedback, we miss opportunities to grow. Sadly, many managers give performance feedback to their direct reports, but can't grow themselves because they do not, in turn solicit feedback from those they seek to influence. As a manager, ask your direct reports, "What do I do well as your manager?" and "What do I need to do differently to be more effective." Remember, it takes a willingness to be somewhat vulnerable if we are to build trust, but the payoffs are well worth it.

If you are curious about the extent to which your colleagues, your boss, or your direct reports view you as trustworthy, you may visit www.ambroseconsulting.com, where you and your colleagues can complete a 360-degree assessment tool called the *Interpersonal Trust Profile*. I developed this self-scoring online instrument to allow you to assess your own trustworthiness on the four dimensions of trust discussed in this chapter, and to get feedback from others as well.

6 The Leader's Character

Several years ago I participated in a planning retreat for the senior staff of a now defunct retail enterprise. The staff wanted to take time to assess their situation, generate some innovative ideas, and lay new plans. On the date of the scheduled event, the CEO declined to participate. After some prodding and cajoling he showed up hostile and visibly beleaguered. I listened aghast as this man whom I knew as an affable community leader, baseball dad, and friend stood up in front of his staff and declared, *"I'm here to make a profit for this company, not to make you feel good, and I really don't care what you think of me, just give me your best efforts so we can turn this thing around. As I see it, the solution to our problem is simple: We just need to learn to act like predators. We need to stalk our competitors and pounce on them—obliterate them."*

Now to some observers this stance might be hailed as a show of bravado and even refreshing honesty. But as the meeting wore on I became aware of the dynamics and the tension in this senior management team. The CEO's singular focus was on blaming his staff for the financial jam they were in. He was unable to look at the entire picture. He denied the fact that the neighborhood in which they were located was declining economically, even though the buildings across the street were long abandoned, and shoppers no longer felt safe after hours. He could not acknowledge that his failure to scan his environment and to anticipate and plan for the effects of change were factors in their declining sales. By emphasizing profits over principles, and consistently putting task before people, the CEO had created a dehumanizing work environment. Morale and motivation remained low throughout the entire organization. No innovative ideas were forthcoming from his staff. Profits continued to dwindle.

In this particular meeting, the staff acquiesced, nodding in approval after his tirade, then criticizing the CEO when out of earshot. Neither CEO nor staff was able to exhibit the character traits needed in times of crisis, such as grace under pressure, the ability to keep a level head, and a willingness to speak face to face and honestly about concerns, rather than backbiting.

I remained intrigued by how different this leader's behavior under duress was from the person I knew him to be. Under pressure his unloved (and unlovable) "shadow" had emerged, creating the Jekyll and Hyde character I was now observing. Later as we debriefed the experience he acknowledged his anger. He told me he had recently begun therapy sessions for anger management and that he saw his staff as "passive-aggressive like my family." This could be true or it could be a projection of his unresolved past on to his staff. In either case, the lesson is this: Until we come to know ourselves and embrace the shadow that lurks within each of us—the unloved control freak, the quivering wimp, or the angry inner child, in this man's case—we run the risk of encountering the very part of us we fear when we least expect it. Under pressure it emerges as an aberrant character flaw that can derail our higher intentions. To avoid being blind-sided thus, we must acknowledge our shadow. Learn to treat it tenderly. Forgive it, and therefore ourselves, for being less than perfect, and even come to know how all aspects of our character—positive and not so positive—define and serve us in the end. Sadly, although not surprisingly, the

CEO in this example eventually lost the trust of his employees and his customers and went out of business.

Understanding Style versus Character

The point of this chapter is this: **character is more important than style** in determining leadership effectiveness. Yet style and character often get confused as one and the same. They are not. According to Piaget and other developmental theorists, our style or personality emerges at an early age and will likely remain the same for a lifetime. What can, and does change as we develop is our *versatility*. Effective leaders often leave the comfort of their "home-base" style, and use a variety of approaches in interacting with others. While your personality may have you feeling most comfortable when focused intensely on a task, to the exclusion of other people, you may need to develop and use good interpersonal skills to build relationships and trust as you lead. Conversely, if your style is innately "people oriented," to be an effective leader you may need to use a more task-oriented approach when the situation calls for that.

There is *no one right style of leadership.* Different styles—different approaches to interacting with and influencing others—will get different results. A command style may be a great short-term approach in addressing a crisis or upholding the law, but used exclusively over time, it can leave people feeling powerless and resentful, and ultimately lead to sabotage or worse. Conversely, an amiable style can be powerful in building relationships and supporting shared leadership and commitment, but the same amiable style used to excess can lead to costly inaction in tough situations. In over twenty years of style-profiling work with lead-

Leadership Styles and Their Impact

Style	Description	Theme	Usefulness	Drawbacks
Command "The General"	Autocratic, directive, nonnegotiable stance	"My way or the highway."	Gets compliance; good during crises—in the heat of battle	Disempowering; excessive use breeds resentment, alienates, stifles creativity; leads to sabotage
Visionary "The Dreamer"	Big-picture, possibility thinker; high ideals	"Follow me to the mountaintop."	Inspires new direction; can transform the ordinary into the extraordinary	If there is no concrete plan—no follow through, is experienced as empty or grandiose
Amiable "The Healer"	Relationship builder	"People come first."	Gets cooperation and team spirit; heals differences; builds trust.	Can be slow to act when "tough decisions" must be made
Consultative "The Collaborator"	Invites input, participative problem solving and decision making	"Give us your best ideas."	Gets consensus or buy-in; surfaces multiple viewpoints for innovation	Not useful if followers lack information or necessary perspective. Backfires if input is ignored.
Charismatic "The Pied Piper"	Winning personality, passionate, daring, mesmerizing, magnetic	"Come be a part of my winning team."	Engages people at the level of passion and purpose; can rally people in difficult times when innovation and transformation are needed	Tendency of charismatic leaders to be self-absorbed, narcissistic, or impulsive, sometimes to the detriment of organizational goals

ers, I have managed to synthesize a long laundry list of various scholars' attempts to classify leadership styles. I find in my work I can readily identify five styles, so these are the ones I discuss: command, visionary, amiable, consultative, and charismatic. But here is an important caveat: there are no pure representations of these. It is possible for one person to embody aspects of each of these styles, or to tactically use each of these styles as they attempt to influence different outcomes. At the same time, I believe we each have a home-base style with which we are most comfortable. I have summarized the five styles, their characteristics, themes, usefulness, and drawbacks on the previous page.

Regardless of style, leaders are people who use their passion, creativity, ideas, and influence skills to challenge the status quo and foster change, and they do so the best way they know how. They are after the same thing: goal attainment. But each does it differently, using different combinations of competencies, style, and character. The quiet, yet shrewd visionary Mahatma Gandhi was an impressive leader; so was the colorful, yet strategic General MacArthur. The warm, self-sacrificial Mother Teresa was a powerful leader; so was the dignified, persistent Shirley Chisholm.

In my work as a management consultant, I often encounter managers who ask me to help them change their **style** of managing; some even speak of finding ways to emulate an outstanding leader they know. The point they often miss is that if they contrive a new style that is inconsistent with their personality, followers have an uncanny ability to detect such behavior as being inauthentic. This will eventually erode trust—a prerequisite for a mutually satisfying work relationship. I tell people they are better off investing their time in self-knowledge, spiritual growth, and character development.

Character has to do with traits: personal, moral, and spiritual. As we learn to reflect on ourselves we become clearer about our values, beliefs, and the character traits associated with these. Regardless of your style, are you honest or dishonest? Do you demonstrate integrity such that your espoused values match your actions? Are you courageous? Are your actions guided by concern for others? Are you trustworthy? What is the moral compass that guides your choices? These are the questions of character that followers ask. These are the traits they seek in leaders.

Again, the journey inward is the pathway to character development. First examine the motives that drive your behaviors. Look at the feelings and attitudes you have about your work, your community, and your family to make sure you are in the right place, doing the right things. Reflect on what your true values are. What are the things you would not give up if forced to make a choice? Ask yourself tough questions like: If my family is my first priority, how come I can't make time for them? Then face the answers honestly, without berating yourself. Maybe you *are* called to embrace your life's work in a way that precludes marriage or family. For you it may be less extreme than for those who are called to walk the path of the mystic—the path of solitude or even celibacy. But don't be afraid to delve inside of the lessons of your life leadership experience. Attend to your gifts. Embrace and develop these fully.

As discussed in Chapter 4, we find our inner leader and deploy her in the context of relationships with others. Character development is not different. Personal mastery requires that we discern the needs and motives of others, and use our self-knowledge to be responsible and responsive in acting on what we learn. Wise leaders listen to what followers seek. With impressive regularity, workers in every sector I have consulted list similar expectations of leaders:

1. **Followers want congruence between your "rhetoric" and your behavior.** In my work with organizations involved in planned change, one of the most demoralizing behaviors (based on employee complaints) is the failure of management to lead by example. "Walk the talk" is now a popular adage touted by disappointed followers who observe would-be leaders listing lofty ideals in their mission statements, while behaving in ways that are contradictory to those values. The net result is a loss of trust that impedes management's ability to engage followers.

2. **Followers want authentic caring, not manipulation or showmanship.** Leaders in all sectors often go after the right changes for the wrong reasons. Often I encounter clients who say: "We need to be less autocratic and promote more employee involvement because then they won't resist the changes we have planned." While involving employees in decisions that will affect them is the right thing to do **most** of the time, it is often done for the wrong reasons. We should involve employees because it honors who they are and what they bring to bear on solving business problems. It is both the right thing and the smart thing to do, from a business perspective. But if it is done simply as a manipulative ploy to avoid employee resistance, it will be perceived as such. If, for example, the manager calls a meeting to ask for input, after having already made the decision (as is often done in organizations), the lack of trust that this engenders is more

devastating than if the manager exercised true leadership: a willingness to tell the truth, in this case that a command decision has been made. The leader's and the followers' needs would be better served by admitting that a top down decision was made. I am convinced that workers would rather be told: "We're doing this because we see it as the only way out," or "Management made this decision under the constraints of our regulators, and it is not negotiable," rather than "We're doing this for your own good," or "Give us your ideas"—after the fact.

3. **Followers want their needs and values to count.** If a leader fails to know his or her followers, the leader loses momentum and fails—unless the followers become convinced that present values and beliefs no longer serve them. This is in fact the greatest leadership challenge for those who undertake major culture change in any organization, even when invited to do so by would-be followers. This is where patience, persistence, competence, and the ability to inspire and lead by example become critical for both leader and followers. If the leader consistently fails to help followers achieve desired results or denies followers their rights and expectations, they will eventually become disillusioned and will remove the leader either by "brute force" or, more often, by noncompliance and lack of commitment. The leader is empowered only so long as he or she understands the followers' needs and motivations.

It is also important to know your followers because, as explained in Chapter 4, followers and leaders are inextricably linked. Honest, ethical, concerned followers demand these qualities in their leaders. Conversely, followers who are dishonest or unethical can reinforce or call forth the same behaviors in their leaders.

4. **Followers seek personal power—the capacity to ensure the outcomes they want.** That's why they seek leaders in the first place. Shared leadership is most effective. Yet, this does not mean that the leader cannot act with conviction. At times the formal leader may be convinced that his or her personal vision holds the best solution for the future. At those times the leader may, through persuasion and example, attempt to negotiate a strong coalition of support for the vision. This is not the same as manipulation or coercion **if the motivation is in the best interests of the followers**. In fact, in many instances, followers seek this "conviction" in a leader. They may ask for clarity of direction, or "strong leadership." At other times, however, the goals of followers should be allowed to supersede the leader's personal bent or at least to modify it. Formal leaders gain greater commitment and better results when they are flexible and responsive. Knowing how to listen and integrate the needs of followers is an art. I am learning that it is not enough to treat people as I would like to be treated. As a leader I must learn to treat people as *they* would like to be treated. Remember, "ownership" is at the heart of a motivated work team.

In developing my own leadership competence I have had to clarify my personal mission, which is *to help us discover the meaning in our work lives in order to create more satisfying results*. I am guided by a belief that all enterprises—business, government, health care, not-for-profit, academic—must learn that it is possible to do well by doing good, and that being an effective and profitable enterprise includes caring about planet Earth and its citizens.

As part of my personal call to leadership, I also want to encourage people to create personal *definitions of success* that take into account our unique character, style, talents, and needs. Doing so gives us clear leverage points from which to transform our jobs into meaningful work, and our lives into a celebration of our unique journey.

As I reflect on the way things are done in most organizations today, I am mindful of the following shifts we could make that would enhance the quality of leadership as we go about transforming ourselves and our work.

From Processing Pain to Celebrating Possibilities

I cringe when I meet with pessimistic managers who are in effect telling their staff, "It's going to be hell getting there, but follow me." I cringe again, when in employee focus groups there is little energy for documenting what *does* work, and an inordinate amount of gusto in recounting all the *"ain't it awfuls."*

The dramatic rise of humor consultants in our workplaces bears further evidence of the loss of spirit and the presence of pain. Our popular media, the mirror of our culture, reinforces this with its focus on bad news as the only news that's fit to print.

It is far too rare these days to encounter people "whistling as they work." This is true among the rank and file, as well as management. Employees are suffering a crisis of lost trust. And they have become more vocal about their pain. A few years ago Delta airline employees confronted senior management for voting themselves robust bonuses while asking employees to take pay cuts. Situations like this challenge formal leaders to examine their character and to become better at doing the right things. In the Delta case, the CEO publicly acknowledged his poor decision, recanted, and offered a public apology.

These occurrences are taking place when many baby boomer senior leaders are facing their personal midlife crises of integrity. Instead of mindlessly climbing the metaphoric ladder past where they might be happiest, some of these formal leaders are seeking spiritual and executive guidance as never before. Through coaching and self-reflection some are even choosing alternate career paths and divesting themselves of material excesses—downshifting their lifestyles in order to be more capable parents, or more effective humans.

Our workplace wounds are many. And they will probably persist for a while until we make the necessary transformations. The pains brought on by change-weariness and losses have created an undercurrent of cynicism and anger that we cannot avoid in our leadership efforts. Since we spend 50 to 70 percent of our waking hours engaged in workplace occupations, a critical aspect of personal leadership has to be that of finding ways to add deeper meaning to that experience for ourselves as individuals and for those whose lives we influence. To restore wellness we will need to pay serious attention to the inner toll of today's organizational life. This brings us to the second necessary shift.

From Anger to Forgiveness

Psychologists tell us that "anger turned inward" can lead to depression, guilt feelings, or feelings of inadequacy. As the philosopher Montaigne put it, "There is no passion that so shakes the clarity of our judgment as anger." If we misman-age anger by directing it inward or misdirecting it at the wrong persons, we create conditions that will make us less effective human beings. Anger directed at ourselves can cause us to procrastinate, make poor decisions, or engage in compulsive behaviors that can become barriers to personal and professional success. Anger aimed at others—family members, coworkers, racial or ethnic groups, and so forth—can damage important relationships or impede our ability to act fairly and humanely.

Brain-imaging research conducted by Daniel G. Amen, M.D., a clinical neuroscientist and psychiatrist, offers some compelling data on what he calls the "mind-soul connec-tion." Among Amen's observations: holding on to anger and past hurts causes an increase in the production of cortisol, the body's stress hormone. Long term, this has devastating physical and emotional effects, including memory loss and a compromised immune system. Forgiveness, he believes, is an important antidote.

This does not mean that leaders do not or should not experience anger. On the contrary, anger has its usefulness. Anger often signals us that something is wrong; that some-thing needs to change. Feeling angry may alert us that our basic needs or values are being affronted. The anxiety caused by anger can motivate us to take positive steps to re-lieve our discomfort and return us to a more contented state. In such cases, anger becomes a catalyst for change—an opportunity to exercise leadership by confronting and working through the circumstances that incited our anger. It does mean, however, that to succeed the leader must learn to express anger appropriately and then release it in order to focus positively on the work ahead.

If, as would-be leaders, we remain consumed with anger at our parents for mistakes they made, or obsessively angry about historical wrongs committed against our ethnic group, or filled with venom about "the system" in which we work, it is less likely that we will be able to respond effectively to the interpersonal and spiritual demands of leadership.

By working through and releasing our anger, we free ourselves emotionally to address the cause of the anger by demonstrating positive, constructive leadership.

In my life's work, I am acutely aware of the racial inequities in the upper ranks of corporate America. As I conduct leadership training seminars, I am reminded daily that racial and ethnic "minorities" (African Americans, Hispanics, Native Americans, Asians) and women are often missing from key decision-making positions in business. My awareness is compounded in a very personal way by some of the mistaken assumptions people make about me based on my race and gender. These personal reminders, innocent though they may be on the part of the individuals involved, trigger my anger.

To remain positive, effective, and caring as a human resource professional, I must daily find ways to practice forgiveness and gratitude for the many privileges I do have. This allows me to view my position as an opportunity to make a positive impact on a less-than-perfect world. In working through anger, I have found the following personal leadership tactics to be helpful:

1. **Acknowledge your feelings of anger.** People who are afraid of "losing control" often deny their anger. The result is often indulgence in passive aggressive behaviors, which in the long run tend to be more destructive than healthily expressed anger.

2. **Diagnose why you are angry, then verbalize it at the appropriate time and place.** In doing this, it is helpful to "befriend" your anger. As Buddhist monk Thich Nat Hahn taught: invite your anger to come sit with you and describe its nature to you. Rather than talking about the person or persons that incite your anger, seek opportunities to simply verbalize that you are angry, and why. Then move on. One of my most cathartic moments in business was the day I spoke my truth in a staff meeting by simply saying, "This makes me angry because . . ." I said it in a simple, declarative statement—no attack, no acrimony, just a simple and very freeing declaration. After a few moments of silence, someone else spoke up and said, "It makes me angry, too." And a whole new and very positive dialogue ensued. Later, one of my mentors taught me to take this to another whole level of personal mastery by taking full ownership of my anger. She taught me to say "*I make myself* angry, when you . . .!" (then describe the behavior).

3. **Understand that not every battle is worth fighting.** The short-term gains of "being right" are often not worth the long-term costs. As Carol Tavris puts it in her book, *Anger*, "Sometime the best thing you can do about anger is nothing at all. Let it go, and half the time it will turn out to be an unimportant, momentary shudder, quickly forgotten."

4. **View anger as a potential motivator for positive change.** I know a highly successful research chemist who chose to become a leader in his field largely because of an incident that made him angry. His high school chemistry teacher insensitively told him that he showed no aptitude in the subject and

should avoid taking any more chemistry courses. He chose the following thought pattern: If I apply myself, surely I can master chemistry. As a result, his **feelings** were those of being challenged, rather than discouraged. The **action** he then chose was to throw himself into a pursuit of the subject, and in the process developed both a great love for it and expertise in it.

5. **Know when and how to use anger strategically** to draw attention to critical issues, then release it in order to address those issues with a clear head. When individuals march in protest, they draw attention to injustices that upset them. To address an agenda for change with those who are the source of their anger, the leadership must then move past the anger in order to direct their energies toward solutions.

6. **Develop the ability to forgive others.** People who harbor long-term grudges do great damage to their own psyches. At the same time they become less effective as leaders. A leader who is consciously or unconsciously motivated by residual anger not only impairs his or her own judgment, but is less able to inspire and motivate others to take positive steps for change. When I meet employees who are unable to work past their anger about their unmet needs in the workplace, I often observe a distortion in the way they interpret even the most "innocent" decision or action of their superiors. If your goal is to hone your leadership skills, it is important to remember the impact of residual anger on our ability to interpret events accurately and make **sound** decisions.

This brings us to a third, important pathway.

From "Nibbling" to Empowerment

People who feel powerless are less capable of empowering others. They hoard information and are less apt to encourage others to fully develop. Leaders at their best share power; they find ways to allow their followers to share the responsibility for creating conditions that are best for the followers and for those whose goals and interests are at stake.

Bob Carpenter, a sales manager in a major electronics firm, is a typical example of how less powerful people operate. Three years ago he hired a new sales representative who turned out to be an exceptionally impressive employee. Not only was Bob's new hire well liked by customers and employees, she routinely broke sales records in her department. Bob's boss noticed, as did everyone else, and he recommended that Bob begin to "groom Barb for a management position."

When I met Barbara Jones, the new sales rep, she had sought me out for counseling because she felt that no matter what she did, her boss, Bob Carpenter, failed to support her. He never acknowledged her excellent performance, withheld key information needed in her job, and began to avoid interacting with her whenever he could.

Because I was employed as a consultant at Bob and Barbara's firm, I had access to input from Bob, Barbara, and several other people who observed this scenario. When I spoke with Bob about his working relationship with Barbara, he said she was "too aggressive" and "power hungry." When I spoke with Bob's colleagues, several insisted that Bob had always felt insecure about his current position and had a history of ignoring the most successful members of his sales force. In fact, he typically devoted most of his time to those who were struggling and less likely to vie for management positions.

Three years later, disillusioned with her experience under Bob's management, Barbara left to join a competitor's firm. She now reported to Donald Butler, another client of mine. I casually asked Donald how Barbara was doing in her new job. His response was, "I think I have found my potential replacement!" He then went on to discuss with great enthusiasm his plans for coaching and grooming Barbara for management. At the end of his conversation with me he added: "You know, I'm developing a real knack for finding good people."

This experience reinforced what I have repeatedly observed about leadership and power: **people who feel powerless may try to minimize the potential of others so they can feel more powerful by comparison**. Kaleel Jamison, in her book, *The Nibble Theory and the Kernel of Power*, wrote: "Many people look at themselves and they look at others and they think that the way to get bigger themselves is to get others down to size, make others smaller. So they start to nibble."

Nibbling takes many forms. It may involve withholding information from others so they are less capable of making sound decisions. Often this kind of nibbling can be seen in the behavior of people experiencing major organizational change. Department X may withhold information from Department Y to protect their power base or turf. Managers may withhold information from subordinates to keep them "subordinated." When faced with the challenges of organizational change, the effective leader involves subordinates by sharing information freely, thereby **empowering** them to act from an informed position. Such an approach engenders creativity and, in the long run, facilitates the transition process.

Another way that people nibble others down to size is to offer only criticism about poor performance while refusing to acknowledge successes. This approach to leadership erodes self-esteem and diminishes the likelihood of sustained high performance.

To tap our leadership potential we must move from nibbling to empowerment. By inviting people to be their best, we nurture personal power and excellence in ourselves and others.

The fourth pathway holds the key to survival in our emerging global economy, marked by unprecedented uncertainty and dynamism.

From Rigidity to Flexibility

Processionary caterpillars travel in long lines, one behind the other, following their leader for great distances in search of food. Jean-Henri Fabre, a French naturalist, once conducted an interesting experiment with these caterpillars. He enticed the leader onto the rim of a large flowerpot. As the followers crowded onto the rim, the leader found himself head-to-tail with the last caterpillar, in a closed circle.

Locked into their instinctive behavior, the caterpillars circled the rim for seven days until each died of hunger and exhaustion, even though there was a large, visible supply of food nearby! The caterpillars' inability to break out of the habit led to their extinction.

Transforming communities, organizations, or ourselves is much like sailing the high seas. You set your sights on the land ahead, but must continually correct your course as you get blown off track. Success usually comes as a result of having a vision of where you would like to go or how you would like your life to be. You must then be able to focus on that vision whether or not your finances permit it, or your parents condone it, or your other commitments compete with it. Paradoxically enough, while our vision remains fixed, our actions must be flexible.

Inflexible entities soon become obsolete. Successful organizations continually change their practices, services, and product lines to adapt to changing customer values, competition, new technologies, and employee needs. Individuals are the same way. In his book, *Transitions: Making Sense of Life's Changes*, William Bridges suggests that our lives are marked by a series of transitions. Our childhood conditioning about how to deal with endings will determine to a large extent how we handle the disorientation, fear, and disenchantment that accompany change.

If we are to become more effective in leading others, we must first develop sound, healthy practices for managing our personal change. As Bridges points out: "In the transition process, we come to beginnings only at the end. It is when the endings and the time of fallow neutrality are finished that we can launch ourselves out anew, changed and renewed by the destruction of the old life-phase."

In addition to being comfortable with personal change, the wise leader must also be sensitive to the impact of change on group dynamics or organizational behavior. It is important to be aware of the following predictable patterns that complicate the change process, preventing people from "letting go" and moving forward.

1. **Everyone, including those who proposed or implemented the change, experiences "loss."** This may be manifested as disorientation, loss of identity, loss of security, uncertainty, or disenchantment. They may feel ambivalent about the future as

they move from what was "known" and comfortable to what is "unknown" and therefore less comfortable.

2. **Change is typically accompanied by a temporary decline in productivity and an increase in anxiety.** This is due to a variety of factors. First, the sense of loss described above is accompanied by a grieving process that may immobilize those involved as they deal with denial, anger, or confusion. Second, change usually requires learning new skills, using new approaches, and building new relationships. This takes time. It also means that for a while participants in the process become less competent than they were under old, familiar conditions. Even the most experienced member of the transition group must deal with feeling "inexperienced" again. Finally, change usually results in more work until (new) order is firmly implemented. This can become a major reason for resistance, especially in organizations where employees felt overworked or understaffed prior to the initiation of the change.

3. **Communication disruptions tend to accompany change.** Sometimes the breakdown in communication is due to poor planning or lack of trust. At other times it is due to the necessary restructuring of roles, relations, and expectations. Communication problems during change can also be linked to the absence of adequate information or skills.

The following attitudes and behaviors typically occur when leaders manage change well:

1. They recognize that every change represents a loss of what was familiar and allow themselves and others time to mourn that loss.

2. They discuss their feelings about the necessary transition openly and encourage others involved to do the same.

3. They look for ways to help everyone—including themselves—regain a sense of control. This may be accomplished by sharing information and involving people in decisions that will affect them.

4. They are clear about the direction in which they want to move and delineate specific goals and expectations in a way that captures the imagination of others.

5. They mobilize followers by providing resources, or creating an environment that encourages followers to be creative about finding resources to facilitate the movement toward goals. Instinctively or by experience, leaders recognize the importance of deploying time, money, talents, skills, and technology to the process of change.

6. They give top priority to communication. They clarify their vision repeatedly, using a variety of media. They share information fully and in a timely fashion. They recognize that communication is a two-way street, so they **listen** to messages accordingly.

The fifth pathway involves new choices in *how* we structure ourselves and engage others.

From Myopia to Inclusiveness

Workplace values are undergoing a dramatic shift that I believe will pave the way for the kind of personal leadership that this book addresses. We are experiencing a shift away from what Peter Block describes in *The Empowered Manager* as "myopic self-interest." According to Block, the myopic patriarchal values of the traditional workplace reinforce our instincts toward upward mobility by emphasizing control and authority as the primary measures of success. New workplace norms are shifting toward alliances that value diversity and service. The payoff is a more "enlightened self-interest." Employees are encouraged to contribute to business goals through individual initiative. Employers are being required to attend to the shifting needs of the workforce and are responding with cafeteria-style benefits packages that meet particular lifestyle needs and people's desire to balance work, leisure, relationships, and so forth. In keeping with these trends, the new workplace is also beginning to create opportunities for people to be more authentic, vocal, and candid. Personal effectiveness and leadership are now linked to:

> **Integrity**—being clear about what we value and making sure that our actions are consistent with what we say is important.
>
> **Courage**—challenging the status and taking risks.
>
> **Engaging, coaching, and supporting** others to exercise shared leadership of the change process.

In short, dominator models of leadership must make room for more inclusive ones. "How to win friends and influence people" is being reframed as "how to build teams," "how to involve employees and value the diversity they bring," and "how to create a motivating environment that celebrates people and their efforts." We are slowly moving from conventional office politics with its emphasis on "dressing for success" and "playing the game" toward "entrepreneurism," "flexibility," "creativity," and "courage."

Old command and control competencies are less favored than new ones that integrate principled negotiation as described by Fisher and Ury in their best-selling book: *Getting To Yes*. Recognizing that in our leadership efforts we operate in a world riddled with conflict, and that, in fact, leadership typically emerges in answer to a conflict, I have come to embrace negotiation competencies as essential to leadership. How can we maintain integrity and goodwill as we seek to influence other people's behaviors? How can we shift from myopic self-interest to take the needs of others into account as we shape outcomes? The answer lies in a willingness to shift our focus so that we attempt to:

1. Reach satisfactory agreements for both parties.
2. Behave in a way that is principled, that does not seek personal gain at another's expense, but instead leaves the relationship intact or enhanced for future dealings.
3. Seek common ground as a way of forming coalitions for mutual agreements.
4. Use fair, objective, mutually agreed-upon criteria to resolve differences.
5. Focus on satisfying important underlying *needs* on the part of both parties.

Approaching leadership from this negotiation mindset truly requires releasing the more coercive "win-lose" stance typical of less effective people. The leader brings about new states or renews old conditions by enlisting or supporting others in the change process. For this more enlightened mindset, it is easier to respond to environmental threats and opportunities. Our life crises and interpersonal differences become the proving ground for our ability to adapt and to lead, implement and manage change. We develop coping skills that allow us to avoid our own "extinction." True leadership occurs at the intersection of our inner transformations and our outer manifestations as we transact with others to change our world.

Self-Reflection

1. What values would you never give up if forced to make a choice?

2. What qualities in your self are you proud of or pleased with?

3. What qualities or behaviors in others really turn you off or repel you? What aspect of these behaviors or qualities might be part of your own "shadow" side?

4. When you get honest feedback from friends, family, and colleagues, what qualities do they say they admire in you? What qualities don't they like?

5. How effectively do you balance secular concerns (such as making money) with deeper values (such as compassion and "right choices")?

6. If you were to choose one aspect of your character for further development, which one would it be?

. . . Human existence is half light and half dark, and our creative possibilities seem strangely linked to that part we keep in the dark. Trying to bring out our creativity in the workplace, we suddenly realize how unwelcoming a professional corporate setting can be to the darker soul struggles of human existence. But simply turning away from these shadows, . . . does not mean that they cease to exist. . . . Sooner or later the trapped energies will emerge and run our lives in unconscious ways.

—DAVID WHYTE,
The Heart Aroused

7 Leadership and Power

> *Personal power is the extent to which one is able to link the outer capacity for action (external power) with the inner capacity for reflection (internal power).*
>
> —JANET HAGBERG, *Real Power: Stages of Personal Power in Organizations*

Some people are uncomfortable with the word "power." This is understandable. It is easy to attach negative connotations to the word because in many ways it has become synonymous with *coercion* or *manipulation.* We speak of "wielding power" and of "power corrupting" people. We often assume that when people use power someone always wins at the expense of another. I find it helpful to make the distinction between "power over" another and "power to accomplish" something. Power can be positive or negative, depending on the source, the character of the person who embodies it, and the way it is applied. When we act ethically and with integrity, when our actions are motivated by a concern for others, we position ourselves to use power in its most positive sense: **to achieve the goals of leadership, or to help people fulfill their needs.**

Power is the fuel that makes leadership possible—that allows us to ensure the outcomes we envision. Our relationship with power—personal and organizational—has everything to do with how we lead. When we are willing to engage in honest self-assessment, to examine our inner dialogue and the attendant feelings and actions, we are well on the path to developing personal power and leadership effectiveness. If we remain conscious and willing participants in the process of personal growth and self-renewal, our relationship with personal and organizational power changes and deepens over the course of our lifetime. Again, as leaders we promote change more effectively when we draw on both our inner source of power (our ability to reflect on ourselves and to glean and apply the wisdom and the courage our life teaches us) and organizational power (our position, expertise, and knowledge).

Inner power includes where we are in our spiritual development; the degree of self-esteem and self-confidence we embody; such personal character traits as honesty, consistency, discipline, and devotion to our life purpose and integrity; the ability to act in ways consistent with our stated values.

Organizational power, on the other hand, is bestowed upon us by virtue of our expertise, titles, rank, socioeconomic status, and so forth. Yet there are persons at high organizational levels who, because they lack personal power or conviction, are unable to exercise leadership. They diminish themselves and their leadership capabilities by failing to develop themselves personally. Most people I work with are fairly clear about ways to develop organizational power. They know the valued courses of study in their field, how to decipher what their company rewards, and, therefore, how to climb the proverbial success ladder. They use this knowledge, sometimes very successfully, to meet organizational goals.

What is more elusive, I find, is how one develops personal power: how to go inside the self to gather up the gems of our life struggles; how to make choices that are consistent with our soul's call, how to make positive contributions based on individual conviction; how to be comfortable with being ourself in the workplace; how to exercise our unique talents for the enhancement of the larger community; how to feel comfortable about speaking our truth, even in situations where this may be inconsistent with the "company line." These abilities set the stage for the emergence of what Hagberg labels "true leadership." By combining this inner power with organizational power, we are better prepared to challenge the status quo, to achieve consistency between beliefs and actions, and to build and maintain credibility with followers.

Our inner dialogue—the thoughts and the questions we live with—and the feelings and actions this self-talk generates are the most important tools of leadership. Because our inner dialogue is influenced by, and influences, our relationship with power, I want to devote this chapter to an examination of the connection between our thoughts, feelings, and actions.

Reflecting on my own relationship with power, I recall a period of my life in which I gained some important insights about myself in relation to power. In my early twenties, as an undergraduate student at Brooklyn College in New York, I spent many hours with college friends in truly inspiring brainstorming meetings (or "rap sessions" as we referred to them then). We were highly motivated and quite innovative in our thinking about ways to address the social and political issues of our time. We generated many ideas on ways to bring more social equity to our college campuses, ways to address pressing Third World issues, solutions for world peace, eradicating hunger, and so forth. I can still remember the frustration that followed when we would move from reasoning to the implementation phase. It always came back to money (which we didn't have), political clout (which we lacked), and credibility (which we hadn't yet earned).

At the time, similar frustrations were mounting in colleges across the United States. These would manifest themselves as campus demonstrations. Everywhere students were banding together in support groups to vent their feelings of anger and hopelessness. There were marches and "sit-ins" and the taking over of dean's offices. There were cries of protest and demands at every turn.

The most important leadership lesson I learned from this experience in the sixties and early seventies is that in the absence of real personal power, would-be leaders will resort to coercion. When people feel powerless, they eventually turn to force—the only form of power they perceive themselves as having. They attempt to lead by inspiring fear. In the short term, this force or coercion may have the positive effect of drawing attention to the issues. Then, if the advocates of change are fortunate enough to attract into their ranks people who have "real power," their cause can be addressed effectively. In our case, if a dean or other formal leader who had courage, clout, or charisma, who shared our conviction and who had money, said, "Okay, let's offer the students the Women's Studies course or the Black Studies course they want," our goal was accomplished. So these early attempts at empowering ourselves taught me an important lesson: The most well-conceived ideas die if we do not have personal and/or organizational power to implement the concept. At the same time, I remain impressed by the power of our inner and outer dialogue. *We truly believed that we were worthy of the changes we sought and that we could use the force of our beliefs to act in ways that would change the world.*

The Power of Thought

In my consulting practice I meet many supervisors, managers, and professionals who lessen their leadership potential by passing the blame upward. They claim: "The system won't let me," or "It's the folks at the top who are blocking our progress." These employees fail to realize that they too are "the system," and that they have a role to play in their personal experience of power. When I counsel employees who give up their power this way, I ask the question: "What do you have to offer that is valuable to your organization?" I get answers like "commitment," "expertise," "ideas," "feedback," "cooperation," and "compliance." Then we can begin the dialogue of how to begin to grow ourselves personally and professionally, armed with this awareness.

Unfortunately, people are not always aware of their potential. It took blacks in Montgomery, and elsewhere, many years and a few courageous trailblazers to finally realize the one thing they had control over—that they could give or withhold—was compliance. When they ceased to comply by boycotting the buses, they empowered themselves to act. There are many instances of oppression and exclusion that we must continue to rise against if we are to create a better world. But for the purposes of this work on our inner journeys, I am primarily concerned with the ways we collude in our own oppression—the ways we disempower ourselves through our patterns of thought.

Truly great leaders think differently about themselves, their situations, and what's possible. Anne Frank's detention by the Nazis is a most extreme example of an attempt at complete disempowerment. But even in her most dire circumstances, she never relinquished her power of thought. As a result, through her inspiring choices in the way she framed her horrific experiences, she continues to exercise leadership, inspiring us to this day.

Recently I have been reviewing the emerging literature on happiness. What I long suspected has been confirmed over and over again by research on the subject. Happiness is more closely linked to what and how we think about our lives than to the actual situations in which we find ourselves. Jean Fritz Chery, a Haitian artist born with no arms, rose to the challenge of his physical disability, becoming an internationally known artist who won the 1981 United Nations' International Year of the Handicapped Artist Award. His success no doubt is tied to his thought patterns. Here is what Chery said to me when I interviewed him at an art exhibit in Pittsburgh several years ago:

> *In a way, I see my handicap as affording me more possibilities. When I get tired of painting with my mouth, I shift to my left foot; when I'm tired of working with my left foot, I shift to my right foot. People with two arms and hands limit themselves. They only paint with one hand. And when that hand gets tired, they stop.*

The Dynamics of Thoughts, Feelings, and Actions

To become our most powerful self requires honest self-examination. We must look at the ways we block ourselves from achieving our goals. One helpful exercise is to pay attention to our **thoughts, feelings, and actions**. The table below gives examples of how disempowering versus empowering thoughts might shape our feelings and therefore our actions.

The journey inward begins with listening to the daily messages we send ourselves when faced with personal or professional challenges. Remember, our thought patterns shape our life choices. More important, they also help shape our subsequent experiences. Thus, the thoughts-feelings-actions dynamic outlined in the table below is a cyclical process. Our inner dialogue evokes feelings, which, in turn, activate behaviors. The way we process the impact of those behaviors creates new thoughts or reinforces old ones.

Our external world (how we deal with challenges and people) is a reflection of our inner world (what we think and feel). If we frequently think, "That can't be done in this company," or "I'm too old to change directions in my life," we create a future shaped by those premises.

	Inner Dialogue	**Feelings**	**Actions**
Disempowering	They won't let me	Helplessness	Inaction; seeking permission
	I'm inferior	Worthlessness	Self-sabotage or seeking validation from others
	I can't make a difference	Insignificance	Complaining and blaming
	It's every man for himself	Isolated; suspicious	Manipulation; withdrawal
	People are basically lazy	Suspicious	Micromanaging; punitive style of supervision

	Inner Dialogue	Feelings	Actions
Empowering	I choose not to	Self-sufficient	Accepting responsibility
	I am enough	Worthy	Self-affirming; healthy choices
	The world is my oyster	Curiosity and wonder	Risk-taking; courageous choices; joy-filled living
	People basically want to do their best	Trusting; expecting high performance	Coaching and supporting
	I can change my world	Anticipation; hope	Personal and organizational leadership

If we think people can't be trusted, then we operate from a position of fear and defensiveness. This usually evokes defensive responses from others, thereby confirming our negative thoughts. Similarly, if we think subordinates will lose respect for us if we reveal that we don't have all the answers, we set ourselves up to fail because by indulging that thought, we are less likely to ask for their help or ideas. We might choose instead to work in the dark—making decisions without the necessary input from the work team.

Public speaking, the number one fear of Americans according to the *Book of Lists*, provides perhaps the best example of this point. A speaker whose thoughts turn to what could go wrong, instead of what would be most useful for his or her audience, is more likely to fail. Often public speakers approach the podium thinking, "I'm going to draw a blank," or "They'll probably ask me questions I can't an-swer." These **thoughts create feelings** of anxiety and self-doubt. These feelings trigger physical symptoms such as tense muscles, shaking hands, a tight throat, and "butter-flies" in the stomach. The resulting **action** lacks focus on the audience's needs as the speaker muses on his or her own stress level. This naturally increases the possibility of drawing a blank, or fumbling through a difficult question to save face rather than admitting to a lack of information on a particular aspect of the topic (which, by the way, audiences can handle if it is done with integrity).

In leadership, as in all other aspects of life, our thoughts motivate our actions. If we concentrate on what could go wrong, we approach leadership from a position of power-lessness. This is a contradiction in terms, since power fuels leadership and leadership breeds power.

When social change advocates fail, it is often because they dwell more on what's lacking than on what's possible. By spending a disproportionate amount of thought energy documenting the difficulties, they leave no energy for envi-sioning and attracting better conditions. After a recent fund-raising dinner for a major civil rights organization, I left feel-ing depressed and hopeless, demotivated rather than "pumped up" for change. The reason? Both the keynote speaker and the executive director of the organization spent their entire speaking time revealing shocking statistics about the blight and hopelessness in our inner cities. While their content was accurate and the issues certainly worthy of at-tention, by focusing only on the negative side of the equa-tion (what is lacking) and omitting the positive side of the equation (what is possible), they created feelings of despair, and were, therefore, unable to sign on new members for their change efforts.

I typically work with organizations that struggle with contemporary challenges like "downsizing" the workforce, or instituting new values such as "total quality" or "customer first." In this work I notice that regardless of the nature of the business—government or industry, educational or non-profit agencies—**employees undergoing change experience a lot of pain**. Their thoughts and feelings run along the same patterns regardless of their job description or position in the organization. Typical thought patterns when faced with change include: "Things will never be the same again, how awful," or "I've seen new programs come and go; they never work," or "Do they (the top management) really know what they're doing?" Many also think: "The status quo (or the "good old days") were better; at least it was familiar and I knew what was expected of me." The feelings that accompany these thoughts include **disorientation, disempowerment, fear, and loss**.

Even in cases where the employees **agree** that the changes are necessary for survival, these thoughts and feelings create behaviors or actions that may hamper the best leadership efforts.

What is most curious, though, is the fact that the very leaders themselves—the "champions" of the change effort, often allow the same patterns of thoughts, feelings, and behaviors to dull their vision and their enthusiasm. This creates a crisis within the crisis of change. Followers expect their leaders to act with courage, clarity, and conviction. However, these are not qualities born of thoughts of powerlessness.

James Kouzes and Barry Posner, in their excellent book, *The Leadership Challenge*, make the point that the difference between managing (maintaining a stable organization) and leading (creating a new state) is that managing aims at "getting people to do," and leadership inspires people "to want to do." As they also point out, no one follows a pessimist. Unless the leader can discourage negative thinking and visualize the best possible future, it is unlikely that he or she can **get others to *want* to go there!**

Modern medicine now acknowledges what we have known for centuries: the mental attitude of patients is a critical factor in the healing process. There is now scientific evidence that positive thoughts actually release hormones that improve our immune system and our psychological outlook. The same healing process applies externally in our organizations when we interact powerfully with others through positive purpose. Keeping fear, anger, and self-doubt within us is destructive. When we learn how to release those thoughts and feelings, we tend to create "healing" environments on our jobs, in our communities, and in our personal relationships.

The leader's internal patterns of thoughts and feelings can be a major force in inspiring positive thoughts, feelings, and followers. Then the art of shared leadership, where all team members align behind a single vision, can be nurtured. The manager who speaks positively to employees about why they matter, sets stretch goals, holds high expectations of people, and uses feedback and coaching to reinforce performance goals, creates a work climate where people believe they can make a difference and reaps the payoffs that come with this mindset.

If as leaders our thoughts center on what is possible, we create for ourselves and our followers visions of a better future. This, in turn, engenders feelings of hope and commitment that will support the actions needed to create that future. **The ability to envision positive outcomes is the**

essence of leadership. The challenge of **the journey inward** is to uproot old thought patterns that inhibit our effectiveness and replace them with new ones.

The questions we live with and the questions we pose to ourselves in the process of the journey inward are also key aspects of our inner dialogue. Whether we are communicating externally (interpersonally) or internally (intrapersonally), question and answer, call and response make for sound dialogue. In the asking and the telling, rich data emerges. We get new awareness; we sharpen our insights and grow toward greater wisdom. At times it is sufficient to simply live with the question for a while. No need to hurry the answer. Just be conscious of the question you are living with or the question that has suddenly appeared to come live with you. These questions, according to Greg Levoy, are related to our "callings." They don't go away but keep reasserting themselves until they are reckoned with. Part of you may say this makes no sense. Another part of you says your life will make no sense without it.

Self-Reflection

Exercise 1

Identify recent success you have had. Pick something that you initiated or contributed to in a major way. Answer the questions below as they relate to the event you identified.

1. What inner dialogue motivated you as you worked on the project?

2. What were your predominant feelings?

3. Describe your actions and your outcomes.

Exercise 2

Reflect on your typical thought and feeling patterns—the typical behaviors you engage in when facing each of the situations described below.

Family Gatherings

THOUGHTS	FEELINGS	ACTIONS

Going to Work Each Day

THOUGHTS	FEELINGS	ACTIONS

Making a Major Purchase

THOUGHTS	FEELINGS	ACTIONS

Expressing Dissatisfaction to Your Supervisor or Hierarchical Leaders

THOUGHTS	FEELINGS	ACTIONS

Expressing Dissatisfaction to Someone You Supervise

THOUGHTS	FEELINGS	ACTIONS

Receiving Criticism from Another Person

THOUGHTS	FEELINGS	ACTIONS

Asking for What You Want, or Wanting More

THOUGHTS	FEELINGS	ACTIONS

Now go back over both exercises and look for themes in your thoughts and feelings. The following questions might help:

1. How did you define "success" in the first exercise?

2. In what kinds of situations do you have positive attitudes? Negative attitudes?

3. What situations create the most stress for you? What kinds of behaviors are typical for you in those stressful situations?

4. How has your inner dialogue shaped your sense of personal power and your leadership behaviors positively and/or negatively?

5. What would you like to do differently as a result of these insights?

8 Dilemmas of Leadership

To be in harmony with all things, you must first be in harmony with yourself.

—*Lakota Proverb*

In today's climate, leadership has become a balancing act. We walk a tightrope towards our visions and goals, juggling the demands of shifting markets, scarce resources, and dazzling changes. As we do so, we confront several dilemmas that can trip us up—dilemmas of leadership. A dilemma is somewhat different from a problem. When a typical problem confronts us, we can use a thought process such as scientific inquiry to solve the problem. We examine its nature. We look at causes and effects. We generate criteria for the solution, and then brainstorm possible solutions, measuring each against the criteria. We implement the chosen solution, and voilà! If we are successful, the problem goes away, hopefully for good.

With a dilemma, on the other hand, no matter what solutions we choose, it creates a new problem that must be reckoned with: We cut jobs to save the company. Operating costs go down, but surviving workers' angst goes up as they face work overload and distrust. Their productivity and creativity suffer, at least short term. This new problem must be managed. Or we take affirmative steps to ensure workplace access for an excluded minority group. Even if the new entrant is the perfect worker, ideally suited for the job, someone somewhere in the organization experiences reverse discrimination and we face a backlash that must now be addressed.

To be successful, enterprise leaders must be adept at juggling endless dilemmas of this sort as goals, needs, expectations, resources, fiefdoms and cultures collide. It takes thoughtful leadership to create harmony out of the chaos of our daily transactions. It requires a particular mindset that is comfortable with the discomfort of paradox. In this chapter, I will outline a series of these dilemmas and paradoxes and offer some suggestions on ways to achieve balance and maintain integrity in the face of each one.

Dilemma 1: **Balancing the need for quick action with the need to engage others.** This dilemma is an important issue in the decision-making process. Basically, there are three approaches at a leader's disposal when making decisions. The first approach is often labeled the **command** approach. Here the leader decides on a course of action and hands down that decision in "take it or leave it" fashion. The advantage of this efficient approach is that it works well when there is a crisis or when the situation dictates no room for negotiation. For example, in most organizations today, safety is never negotiable; the organization surveys its environment and develops a safety policy. Participants who adhere to the policy continue to be part of the organization and those who don't face punitive actions or may no longer be part of the organization. The term "command decision" obviously comes from military jargon. In the heat of battle, a strong, decisive leader acts. Where there is much at stake, when people are in danger, followers expect the leader to act quickly in a forthright manner.

There are disadvantages to the command approach when applied inappropriately. It alienates people and does not allow for innovation. In situations calling for creativity, it would be an inappropriate option as it is limited by not incorporating the various views of people who may have expertise to lend to the decision-making process.

The second available option is called the **consultative** approach. This may be used in two ways. When the leader asks for input among followers but reserves the right to use or not to use that input, depending on the restraints that the leader may face, he or she uses the consultative approach. In using this approach, it is very important for the leader to make ground rules clear to the followers. Perhaps one of the most frequent mistakes in business meetings occurs when the leader gives the impression that he or she is gathering information in this consultative mode—that he or she wants the input and will use it—when, in fact, the leader has already made a tentative decision. The leader may then, upon receiving input, try to change the participants' view so that it fits the tentative decision already made. This, of course, alienates people and poorly executes the consultative approach.

A second, consultative, approach engages participants in joint decision making. This means that the leader elicits input, while indicating a willingness to be flexible on his or her position so the group can capitalize on its collective intelligence and experience. The advantages of using this consultative method are threefold. First, people feel included and thus are more likely to commit to carry forth the decision. Second, the leader benefits from having the added input of those with direct-line responsibility for areas within the leader's responsibility. The consultative method supports today's changing business climate because it also builds participatory involvement and team spirit.

The third approach to decision making is the **consensus** approach. This is where the leader says to the group, "Let's deliberate until we all reach agreement on the preferred course of action." While time consuming and often difficult to achieve, this approach is useful where significant agreement or buy-in is required. Consensus decision making goes beyond just collaboration to inspire workers to "own" the problem, "own" the solution, and therefore have a larger stake in the organization and its outcomes. There is rarely such a thing as 100 percent consensus. Leadership of consensus seeking may mean that everyone has had a chance to give their input, and those who don't fully agree are willing to go forward, having had their say. It is important to hold out for some form of consensus in situations where the stakes are high and risks could be costly.

All three approaches, command, consultative, and consensus, have their place in the leadership process. The dilemma for the leader is in deciding when to command and when to engage others. How does a leader make this decision?

First of all, size up the situation and decide whether it represents a crisis. Ask for input from followers about what they perceive is needed in the situation. Often followers say to the leader, "We need you to make the decision. We need you to tell us what to do. We need you to be decisive and authoritative at this moment." At other times, followers say, "We need to express our feelings; we need to have input." So this decision making is an important step to take. Related to that step, leaders must ensure that once they decide which of the three decision-making approaches to use, they communicate that approach to the followers. Followers can handle it if, for example, they are told, "This is going to have to be a command decision; my hands are tied by the regulators," or "We're going to have to do this; it's the law." If, on the other hand, the leader says to the followers, "We're going to go the consultative route. I need your input and your ideas. I will work very hard to incorporate them," that too can be accepted if clearly expressed.

When delegating to followers, the leader must be sure to stipulate the delegated assignment and outline the degree to which it is delegated. In other words, does the leader want them to take the ball and run with it and not seek input at all unless there is a problem, or are they to periodically check with the leader to give progress reports, or are they fully responsible for the outcome? Again, if stated clearly, people can handle it. They know what is expected of them and will carry out the decision in a much more concrete way.

Finally, leaders must recognize that leadership doesn't work at one end or the other of a continuum, but moves freely up and down the continuum. The wise leader analyzes the risks involved, the skill level of the individuals, the situation itself, and then, based on that analysis, chooses the command, consultative, or consensus route for the situation. The command approach gets compliance while the consultative or consensus approach can inspire commitment.

To make the appropriate decision-making choice with integrity means being clear about available choices, being clear about your intentions as the leader, and being honest and open to your followers about your actions. If you do this consistently, then, in most cases, you will get the support of coworkers whenever faced with this dilemma of choice.

Dilemma 2: **Do more, faster, better—with fewer resources and less time.** It is safe to say that almost all of us work in a climate where, for various economic reasons, we are called upon to do more with less. As organizations become leaner, competition becomes fiercer and resources become scarcer; today's leader faces the challenge of balancing personal vision with limited resources. This dilemma calls forth a great deal of creativity and resourcefulness if the leader is to succeed in achieving goals. To attain his or her vision, the leader must encourage others to find new ways to reduce costs and to reach goals in the absence of sufficient financial and human resources.

Specifically, leaders must redefine how they view human resources. Training and joint decision making become key variables in creating a workforce adept and flexible in carrying out multiple functions where necessary. This may require a major shift in priorities for leaders reluctant to develop the talents of workers.

Dilemma 3: Do things right and do the right things. Earlier I discussed the differences between managing and leading, citing the work of Warren Bennis and Burt Nanus and their often quoted, "Managers are people who do things right, and leaders are people who do the right thing." In pointing out this distinction, the authors also indicate one of the most trying leadership dilemmas: leaders struggle to understand how "doing things right"—acting efficiently, rewarding behavior consistent with goals, and discouraging or punishing behaviors that aren't—combines with "do the right things"—having the courage to upset the apple cart of stability in order to risk moving in bold new directions.

Doing the right things is the essence of leadership. It involves experimenting and challenging the status quo in order to foster innovation, find new ways to nurture breakthrough ideas, answer discontent among the workforce, or challenge the competition. Sometimes this means *not* doing things right, not going by the historical book. The courage to do the right thing requires that we make tough choices: whether to go out on a limb alone, how far out on the limb to go, or what to do if the risk causes failure. My former mentor Ron Greene taught me to ask clients, "What risk are you willing to take to be a more effective leader?"

Ralph Dickerson, president of the United Way of New York City, in talking about some of the more challenging leadership dilemmas of his career, sums up his understanding of how to resolve this "tug and pull" of managing versus leading, saying that when you take on a leadership role you must be "willing to be measured by the actions that you take." According to Dickerson, "You aren't leading if you aren't risking. When someone tells me I'm taking a risk by trying this path, I say, 'What else am I supposed to be doing?'" Dickerson goes on to explain that once he makes the decision to do what in his mind is the "right thing," he then relies on his staff, working in partnership with the community and the funding sources, to manage the effort by doing things right.

Dilemma 4: **Balancing long-term goals with short-term progress.** This is an important dilemma for leaders to think about because in leading a change effort, it is not unusual for those targeted by the change and for those involved in seeing the change through to become disillusioned or frustrated if they are not able to see immediate results of their efforts. The wise leader understands this dilemma and plans "small wins," as they have been called in the literature on management and leadership training. That is, the leader sees to it that there are incremental steps taken toward the larger goal. The leader communicates, "We're going to go from A to Z, but first let's concentrate on getting from A to B, from B to C, and so forth." At each step along the way, the leader remembers to celebrate those successes so that all persons involved in the change effort get a sense of progress and gain momentum with each success. Thus morale is less likely to be diminished, commitment is maintained, and the task does not seem so overwhelming that it saps the energy level and the spirit of the participants in change.

What makes this dilemma a difficult one today is the fact that many of us are so busy fighting short-term fires that there is little energy left at the end of day to engage in the sort of transformative thinking for the future.

***Dilemma 5:* Balancing "tradition" and diversity.** This is a relatively new dilemma of leadership, brought on by shifting workplace demographics and by the recognition that most organizations have not yet succeeded in creating a climate where all members are valued and empowered to perform to their best capacity. In fact, many in the field of leadership development would contend that our inability to create inclusive work cultures that value diversity in perspectives and backgrounds has contributed to the steady decline of productivity over the past two or three decades. Many leaders who confront the dilemma of managing and valuing diversity find that their lack of experience and sophistication in dealing with the social distance between people who are different from each other impedes their ability to effectively motivate others and develop good interpersonal work relationships. One of the serious organizational consequences of this is that many minorities are not adequately included. As a result, they cannot develop and contribute all they are capable of bringing to the workplace.

The resulting lack of trust and presence of awkwardness presents problems of both productivity and creativity for minority and majority team members alike. To better manage this dilemma, today's leaders must develop skill in working effectively with people whose gender, culture, race, sexual orientation, socioeconomic background, or physical capabilities differ from their own. The challenge for the leader is to free himself or herself from operating out of a biased or stereotypical frame of reference. Because leaders are by definition "people in power," it is easy for them to slip into feeling comfortable with the status quo. Thus, they can easily avoid raising difficult issues related to differences or to the needs of people who are not empowered or not "in power." A leader's refusal to address these issues prevents followers from fully participating in the leadership agenda.

In the words of R. Roosevelt Thomas, Jr., executive director for the Institute for Managing Diversity at Atlanta's Morehouse College, "In a country seeking economic advantage in a global economy, the goal of managing diversity is to develop our capacity to accept, incorporate, and empower the diverse human talent of the most diverse nation on earth. It's a reality. We need to make it our strength."

***Dilemma 6:* Balancing the tension between ego and goals.** Because we're human, we all live with the polarity of **ego** versus **goals**: "looking good versus doing good." For example, if you were raised in an environment where you were constantly pressured by an overbearing or dominant parent, you may have developed an ego mechanism for coping with the anxiety that those behaviors triggered. You may have learned to "tune out" the dominating parent. This behavior, as it gets transferred from situation to situation in order to protect your ego needs, would then be exhibited later in life to *anyone* who came on as strong, aggressive, or overbearing. So in the workplace or in a leadership context you might respond to a domineering colleague or subordinate using the same defense mechanism of tuning them out.

This implies then that a major challenge of leadership is self-analysis, aimed at identifying the potential blind spots of our ego's needs that get in the way of our being most effective and responsive in the leadership role.

Dilemma 7: **Harmonizing expediency with right choices.** Leaders are routinely challenged by having to balance the polarities of profits and ethics, efficiency and effectiveness, and concerns for task with concerns for people. In their groundbreaking book *Essentials of Business Ethics,* Madsen and Shafritz remind us: "The expedient decision always has hidden costs." The past three decades have given us many glaring examples of the hidden costs incurred because of leadership's inability to manage these polarities well. The most notable of these include the Enron scandal of the 1990s, the O-rings disaster which caused the space shuttle Challenger's crash in the 1980s, and the Ford Pinto case of the 1970s which resulted in a company being found guilty of "corporate murder" for the first time in history.

These days, e-businesses raise new ethical dilemmas related to privacy and the rights of ownership. According to an InformationWeek survey, 62% of companies monitor employees' web-site use, 60% monitor employees' phone use and 54% monitor employees' email in an attempt to curtail unethical workplace practices. In fact, some companies now employ Chief Privacy Officers (CPOs)—senior level executives whose job includes enforcing business ethics policies. And industry leaders like Johnson & Johnson review and update their values statements and codes of conduct regularly, all in an attempt to exercise good leadership in managing the moral mazes and dilemmas associated with business and ethics.

We are reinventing work and redefining leadership for the twenty-first century. We are redesigning our enterprises so they are faster, flatter, more flexible, and hopefully more friendly. In the words of Alan Webber, publisher of the business magazine *Fast Company,* we must also see to the "marriage of the soft stuff and the hard stuff." My organization development colleagues like to say, "The soft stuff *is* the hard stuff."

These and other dilemmas remind us that character development through introspection was never more important. Our world has become more complex and more perplexing as geographic boundaries melt away and technology offers up its gifts and its challenges. The dilemmas of our organizations are mirrored in the lives of its individuals. Corporate and government downsizing has a counterpart in individual downshifting of lifestyles and expectations. When institutions feel powerless in the face of change, individuals feel personally less powerful as well. Since 1989, I have surveyed several thousand participants in my leadership seminars. Two questions I ask are: "What are your most pressing concerns as you prepare for leadership?" and "How do you define success?" The answers are by now fairly predictable:

∞ Maintaining morale while dealing with uncertainty and change

∞ Finding time to reflect and make conscious choices

∞ Dealing with issues of lost trust and loyalty

∞ Feeling like what I do matters

∞   Holding my personal life together

∞   Having reasonable control of my work and my life

∞   Having meaningful work that's fun

As challenging as these concerns may sound they belie some very exciting possibilities. For me, this means we have turned our attention to the softer stuff of leadership. We want to ensoul our work with deeper meaning. We want to renew the spirit of our workplaces and our lives. Perhaps this is the greatest gift of today's leadership climate.

Self-Reflection

1. What is the most pressing dilemma you face today in your work? In your personal life?

2. Dilemmas prompt us to make a choice between two competing priorities. This means we must some-times give something up. What are you willing to give up to move closer to where you want to be?

3. In wrestling with the dilemmas you face, what does your mind tell you to do? What does your heart tell you to do?

4. What changes might you make to keep what's important to you in the forefront?

9 Accepting the Leadership Challenge

A dragon was pulling a bear into its terrible mouth.
A courageous man went and rescued the bear.
There are such helpers in the world, who rush in to save
anyone who cries out. Like Mercy itself,
they run toward the screaming.

And they cannot be bought off.
If you were to ask one of those, "Why did you come
so quickly?" he or she would say, "Because I heard
your helplessness."

Where lowland is,
that's were the water goes. All medicine wants
is pain to cure . . .
Be patient.
Respond to every call that excites your spirit.

Ignore those that make you fearful and sad,
that degrade you back toward disease and death.

—RUMI

Leadership is an act of service. Rugged individualism, a cherished value in American society, can cause us to forget that leaders ultimately serve others. The inner journey described in this book prepares the leader to build necessary coalitions or leadership teams to further that service. Private and public sector entities alike are beginning to realize what distinguishes successful organizations is their orientation to service. Organizational success follows when we combine the right people with a strategic vision that takes into account the **needs** of the customer, constituents, employees, and other stakeholders. People Express Airlines failed when it departed from its original focus on exceeding the expectations of customers who were willing to forgo traditional perks for a great price. When they shifted their attention to a different, less loyal customer base they folded. Federal Express, in contrast, propelled itself into success by creating a culture driven by an almost obsessive focus on customer service and conscious attention to the stated needs of the customer.

Great leaders care deeply about humanity and balance heart and head in their dealings with others. When I ask trainees in my leadership seminars to share their stories of the heroes and heroines in their personal and work lives, they rarely start with traits like "decisiveness," "aggressiveness," or being "in control." Yet these are the traits that are most often rewarded in management circles. Instead, with impressive regularity, in describing their most admired leaders, people first latch on to the human traits: "integrity," "caring," "supportive," "a good listener," "a good sense of humor," "trustworthy," "courageous," and "inspirational." If they were coached or mentored by their chosen hero or heroine, they always add with nostalgia: "This person believed in me."

In the discussion that ensues, trainees later admit that they also expect leaders to demonstrate other traits like decisiveness, good planning skills, and competence. But it is the "human" traits that set the great leaders apart from the mediocre and the leaders' ability to balance these traits with other tasks and interpersonal competencies. They are capable of being aggressive, yet fair; decisive, yet flexible (where appropriate); critical, yet caring; emphatic and persuasive in advocating their beliefs, yet able to listen and incorporate input from others. Ancient Taoism, and Judaic and Christian religions, as well as great philosophers throughout history, have all taught the importance of this sort of balance. When Kenneth Blanchard and Spencer Johnson's *The One Minute Manager* became perhaps the most widely read management guide, it was partly because it reaffirmed this universal truth so simply and convincingly. The promise? Tough, but nice; praise with reprimand; clear, firm goals and hard work with a sense of humor; and a belief that all people are potential winners. Perhaps business is beginning to realize that it has lost its heart, and that it must now lose its head to empty itself for a more balanced rebirth. We have focused excessively on the management side of leadership—driven by aggression, analysis, and control—for decades. We are beginning to shift our focus to the human side of leadership: service, employee involvement, team building, trust, and flexibility. This brings us to the next consideration.

Leadership development is both practical and spiritual in nature. Leadership arises out of the practical need to address the everyday crises and challenges that accompany life. At the same time, leadership is about high ideals, creative pursuits, and "visionary" thinking. Many of us now believe that true leadership has a strong spiritual component and that preparation for effective leadership must involve attention to the soul of the leader. Our organizations are only as good as the people who run them. We must continually examine our character and our motives for leading if we are to shape our own and others' lives for the better. One of the most responsible tasks we face as leaders is that of promoting values. At the heart of most leadership initiatives is culture change. The human resource manager charged with changing the way employees are developed and rewarded affirms new values as he or she leads the change effort. The operations manager who decides to approach the bargaining unit with greater trust espouses new values in his or her leadership role, as does the community leader who rallies citizens to march in protest past city hall, or the news editor who decides how to spin the latest event.

In each of these cases, there is a good chance that there will be vigorous debates among different constituents on whether the right values are being promoted. Being spiritually attuned as a leader better equips us to strike a balance between concern for goals and concern for humanity. In one situation, the right thing may mean holding on to our conviction and forging ahead, prepared to pay the price for what we believe is right. In another situation, it may mean accommodating the needs of others. In either case, our clarity of values and purpose, and the spiritual dimension of our personal and professional growth will make the difference.

Not surprisingly, there is a business and consciousness movement afoot in the United States and globally. This has been sparked by workplace turmoil and fueled by disturbing news of insider trading, scandalous government contracting practices, questionable accounting practices, and so forth. This movement, interestingly enough, brings together coalitions from different sectors of the community—schools, government, and corporate America—to promote social responsibility and ethics in every sector. And it coincides with a renewed interest in our inner lives. According to Gallup polls, the number of people who said they felt a desire for greater spiritual growth jumped from 56 percent in 1984 to 82 percent in 1999. Not surprisingly, a business and consciousness movement has taken off. This year so far I have been invited to 24 "Spirituality and Business" conferences worldwide. The business book sections of bookstores now boast best-selling titles like *God Is My CEO*, and *Take Your Soul to Work*.

Leadership is not defined by gender. The competencies and traits needed for effective leadership are the same for both genders. At the same time, there are significant differences in the way men and women are socialized in most, if not all, cultures. From their relative subcultural perspectives, men and women can make complementary contributions to leadership. For decades, management books taught us about very effective "masculine" models of management. This was appropriate since almost all major organizations were headed by men who brought to the workplace the biases of their acculturation into manhood. The masculine models of management and leadership that appeared in our texts were based on the "warrior archetype," which rewarded such behaviors as decisiveness, aggressiveness, and "left-brain" logic. As Sally Helgesen points out in her book, *The Female Advantage*, traditionally feminine characteristics such as "nurturing, mercy, participating in the growth of others, fostering human connection . . . were all qualities that the warrior could not afford to indulge or explore, lest they weaken his resolve to compete. Thus the private domestic sphere over which women reigned became the repository of humane and caring value, while the world of work and politics flourished by ruthless competition."

In more recent years, however, we have added to our understanding of leadership by including "feminine" models of leadership as well. The works of the late Alice Sargent, and Carol Gilligan, Judy Rosener, and Sally Helgesen, for example, document the behaviors of women in the workplace who hold positions of power and leadership. This is timely, given the influx of women into the workplace and into leadership positions over the past twenty years.

These studies provide compelling evidence that, like men, women enter the workplace with their own set of values and acculturation. For many women, this model of being nurturing, supportive, cooperative, and humane—**if allowed to surface**—can be a powerful tool of leadership, especially given our growing orientation toward team building, employee involvement, ownership, and customer service.

But not all women feel confident enough to allow these traits to surface at work. On the contrary, many women feel that to be included they must learn to be "one of the guys." Also, not all women have been socialized in traditional "feminine" values. Many are quite comfortable and effective working with the "masculine" models of leadership. In fact, during the '60s and '70s when women first began to enter the workplace in large numbers, they more or less emulated male models of leadership, regardless of their personal orientation. Some went to great lengths to become clones of men in their dress, demeanor, and approach to work. While this may have been necessary as a transition phase for women, it is no longer the chosen mode. We see a reversal of this trend as women become more comfortable with personal power and leadership roles.

The two viable models of leadership together form a more total picture and raise the possibility that **men and women can learn valuable lessons of leadership from each other in today's workplace**. **Together as men and women, we create meaningful synergy** at work if we value the specific orientations we bring. Most important, if, as individuals, whether male or female, we allow ourselves to be who we are, we incorporate those parts of ourselves that have been repressed by social conditioning. Thus, men can learn to value their intuitive, nurturing, humane side; while women can value the role of assertiveness, vision, and decisive strategy in the total structure of leadership. Through this balance we can all be heroic as we address life challenges at home, at work, and in our communities.

Leadership development is a lifelong process. Our lives chronicle unfolding events, each with its special challenge, each with a special lesson—if we pay attention. This does not mean waiting passively for things to happen, however. In developing ourselves for leadership, we must actively seek out new experiences. Educators are becoming more aware of the need to begin leadership development in schools. In fact, leadership courses and hands-on leadership retreats are now part of the curriculum in more progressive schools. Corporations have long understood the importance of workplace learning in succession planning and human resource development. Currently, employee training and development in industry represents over $200 billion per year. Each major initiative—such as total quality, employee involvement, or customer service improvement—is bolstered by intensive training experiences designed to empower employees to take the lead in guaranteeing the anticipated outcomes. Likewise, performance management and career development strategies move employees into the right series of positions, giving exposure to personal and work-related experience that calls forth their best skills and leadership capabilities.

Purpose and trust are important cornerstones of effective leadership. This is true regardless of our gender, age, place of origin, race, or socioeconomic status. Purpose deals with conviction and the right goals. Trust is earned when we act in people's best interests, demonstrate consistency between what we say is important and what we do, speak honestly, and meet our goals competently. "Right" purpose and trust are also linked to honesty and a willingness to modify our position when proven wrong. Through introspection and assimilation of the lessons of our experiences, each of us discovers our **purpose**. As we learn what specifically we have to offer our communities where we live and work, **we must take steps to ensure that we carry forward our purpose with "trustworthiness."** This means we must continually journey inward to develop our self-esteem and clarify our values so that our leadership choices are guided by a clear sense of purpose and deep wisdom.

Travel lightly.
Enjoy the journey!

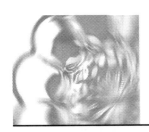

References

Ambrose, Delorese, Ed.D. *Healing the Downsized Organization*. New York, NY: Random House, Inc., 1996.

Axelrod, Richard H. *Terms of Engagement: Changing the Way We Change Organizations*. San Francisco, CA: Berrett-Koehler Publishers, Inc., 2002.

Barks, Coleman with John Moyne, translators. *The Essential Rumi*. San Francisco, CA: Harper Collins Publishers, 1995.

Bennis, Warren and Burt Nanus. *Leaders*. New York, NY: Harper & Row, 1985.

Blanchard, Kenneth and Spencer Johnson. *The One Minute Manager*. New York, NY: William Morrow and Company, 1981.

Block, Peter. *The Empowered Manager*. San Francisco, CA: Jossey-Bass, Inc., Publishers, 1987.

Bridges, William. *Transitions: Making Sense of Life's Changes*. Reading, MA: Addison-Wesley, 1980.

Covey, Stephen M. R. *The Speed of Trust: The One Thing That Changes Everything*. New York, NY: Free Press, 2006.

Depree, Max. *Leadership is an Art*. New York, NY: Doubleday, 1989.

Ferguson, Marilyn. *The Aquarian Conspiracy*. Los Angeles, CA: Jeremy P. Tarcher, Inc., 1980.

Friedman, Thomas L. *The World Is Flat: A Brief History of the Twenty-first Century*. New York, NY: Picador, 2007.

Fritz, Robert. *The Path of Least Resistance: Learning to Become the Creative Force in Your Own Life.* New York, NY: Random House, Inc., 1989.

Gardner, John W. *Leadership Papers, 1–12.* Washington, DC: Independent Sector, Leadership Studies Program, 1986–1988.

Harman, Willis, Ph.D. and Howard Rheingold. *Higher Creativity.* Los Angeles, CA: Jeremy P. Tarcher, Inc., 1984.

Hagberg, Janet O. *Real Power: Stages of Personal Power in Organizations.* Minneapolis, MN: Winston Press Inc., 2002.

Helliwell, Tanis. *Take Your Soul to Work.* Holbrook, MA: Adams Media Corp., 1999.

Jamison, Kaleel. *The Nibble Theory and the Kernel of Power.* New York, NY: Paulist Press, 1984.

Julian, Larry S. *God Is My CEO.* Avon, MA: Adams Media Corp., 2001.

Kanter, Rosabeth Moss. *The Change Masters.* New York, NY: Simon & Schuster, 1983.

Kelley, Robert E. *The Gold Collar Worker.* Reading, MA: Addison-Wesley, 1985.

Kouzes, James M. and Barry Z. Posner. *The Leadership Challenge, 4th Ed.* San Francisco, CA: Jossey-Bass Publishers, 2007.

_____. *Encouraging the Heart: A Leader's Guide to Rewarding and Recognizing Others.* San Francisco, CA: Jossey-Bass Publishers, 1999.

Levinson, Daniel, et al. *Seasons of a Man's Life.* New York, NY: Ballantine, 1979.

Madsen, Peter, Ph.D. and Jay M. Shafritz, Ph.D. *Essentials of Business Ethics.* New York, NY: Meridian, 1990.

Maxwell, John C. *The 21 Indispensable Qualities of a Leader: Becoming the Person Others Will Want to Follow.* Nashville, TN: Thomas Nelson, Inc., 1999.

Millman, Dan. *Living on Purpose: Straight Answers to Life's Tough Questions.* Novato, CA: New World Library, 2000.

Naisbitt, John and Patricia Aburdene. *Reinventing the Corporation.* New York, NY: Warner Books, Inc., 1985.

Reina, Dennis S. and Michelle L. Reina. *Trust & Betrayal in the Workplace: Building Effective Relationships in Your Organization.* San Francisco, CA: Berrett-Koehler Publishers, Inc., 2006.

Sargent, Alice G. *The Androgynous Manager.* New York, NY: AMACOM, 1983.

Schein, Edgar H. *Organizational Culture and Leadership.* San Francisco, CA: Jossey-Bass, Inc., Publishers, 1985.

Tichy, Noel M. and Mary Anne Devanna. *The Transformational Leader.* New York, NY: John Wiley & Sons, 1986.

Wheatley, Margaret J. and Myron Kellner-Rogers. *A Simpler Way.* San Francisco, CA: Berrett-Koehler Publishers, Inc., 1996.

Whyte, David. *The Heart Aroused.* New York, N.Y.: Doubleday, 1994.

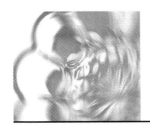

Index

Managers, leaders and, 56,
140–141
Managing
changing style of, 97
vs. leading, 11–27
work and time, 75–76
Manipulation, 119
Material concerns, harmonizing
with spiritual concerns,
144–146
Meir, Golda, 15, 24
"Mind-soul connection" (Amen),
104
Minorities, entrepreneurial
ventures of, 6
Mistakes, admitting, integrity and,
79–80
Moses, 15
Mother Teresa, 15, 97
Motivation
of leaders, 53–54, 59–60
of others, 61–67
self-reflection on, 59, 67–69
taking action and, 60–61
trusting leadership and, 71
Murray, Sandra, 17
Myopia, 113–116

N

Nanda, B. R., 22
Nanus, Burt, 56, 140
"Negative" feedback, 90
Neoteny, 85
*The Nibble Theory and the Kernel
of Power* (Jamison), 109
Nibbling, 108–110
Nicolosi, Richard, 65–66
Nightingale, Florence, 15

O

The One Minute Manager
(Blanchard and Johnson), 151
Opportunities, feedback and, 91
Organizational goals, 67
Organizational power, 120
Organizations
culture audit of, 35
dilemmas of leadership in,
135–136, 145
leading and transformation of,
30–34
successful, 111

P

Parks, Rosa, 17, 20–21, 26
Patton, George, 24
People Express Airlines, 150
"People oriented" style, 95
Perot, H. Ross, 24
Persistence, as component of
motivation, 61, 63, 67
Personal power, 101
developing, 120–121
lack of, 120, 122
Personal struggles, leaders and,
18, 19
Picasso, Pablo, 24
Pittsburgh Paint and Glass (PPG),
25–26
Political agenda, family issues in,
6–7
Posner, Barry, 9, 56, 61, 128
Potential awareness, 123–124
Power
Ambrose relationship with
power, 121–122
definition and types of power,
119–120
dynamics of thoughts,
feelings, and actions,
124–130
organizational, 120
personal, 120–121
self-reflection on, 130–134
of thought, 123–124
Prisons, as new growth industry,
7
"Process theorist", motivation
and, 63–64
Procrastination, 75
Productivity, change and, 112
Product quality, 4–5
Progress
balancing goals with, 141–142
cost of, 7
Promises, integrity and, 79
Purpose, effective leadership and,
155–156

Q

Qatkins, Sherron, 25

R

Rank-and-file workers, 64
Reagan, Ronald, 17

Biography and Contact Information

Since 1982, Dr. Delorese Ambrose has shared her inspiring messages on emerging workplace issues in conferences and seminars internationally. Founder of Ambrose Consulting & Training, LLC, a firm dedicated to personal mastery and organizational effectiveness, Delorese provides coaching and training for clients such as Alcoa, KPMG, Brigham and Women's Hospital, and the U.S. Treasury Department.

She is author of three books: *Leadership: The Journey Inward*, *Healing the Downsized Organization* and, *Making Peace with Your Work: An Invitation to Find Meaning in the Madness*. She has also authored chapters on managing change for two medical textbooks: *Comprehensive Respiratory Care*, and the award-winning *Nursing Management: Principles and Practice*.

Delorese earned a Doctor of Education degree from Columbia University in 1979, and was adjunct Professor of Management at Carnegie Mellon University for eighteen years. She is currently a faculty member of the Institute of Management Studies (IMS) where she lectures throughout the U.S. and in Canada, Amsterdam, Brussels, London, Manchester, and Scotland.

FOR INFORMATION about Delorese Ambrose's seminars and educational products, VISIT:
www.ambroseconsulting.com.

TO BOOK Delorese Ambrose as a keynote speaker VISIT:
www.leadingauthorities.com.